ADVANCE PRAISE FOR *THE LEADER'S VOICE*

"I've read virtually every book on leadership in the past twenty years, and I consider *The Leader's Voice* to be one of the best I've ever read. It's a 'must read' for anyone who has to motivate and inspire others to perform at levels not easily attainable or even imaginable in today's demanding workplace."

—Harry Rhoads, CEO, Washington Speaker's Bureau

"Clarke and Crossland have written an exceptional book. They use clear language and vivid examples to show that leaders who communicate with clarity, passion, and authenticity can significantly raise the level of organizational performance. The stories about the leaders who shaped LensCrafters and TNT are especially worthwhile for those who want to learn how to 'walk the talk.'"

—Oren Harari, Author,
The Leadership Secrets of Colin Powell
Professor of Management, Graduate School of Business
University of San Francisco

"Communication is nothing but the transfer of emotion. Boyd and Ron understand this in their bones. Do you?"

—Seth Godin, Author, *Survival Is Not Enough*

"The role of leadership in any organization includes a careful articulation of why its associates should follow and join in the vision. This book helps you fashion the message, not make the message fashionable. It's a blueprint for why management teams are superior. Whatever skills one brings to the table, the mastery of the three channels of communication requires a strategic importance to the teamwork between marketing, finance, operations, and human resources, so a consistency develops among all the spokespersons."

—Lauren Patch, CEO, Wyncom, Inc.

"Drawing on both historical events and modern-day anecdotes, Clarke and Crossland reveal their secret recipe for innovative leadership—and all its essential ingredients. Virtually anyone who practices or aspires to leadership can find inspiration here."

—Tom Kelley, General Manager, IDEO,
Author, *The Art of Innovation*

"Leadership is the skill most lacking in corporate America, yet the hardest to teach. Clarke and Crossland have taken a giant step forward in showing the way true leaders lead. The rich content, anecdotes, and supporting case studies make it a 'must have' for aspiring and existing leaders alike."

—Alex Brigham, CEO, Corpedia Education, Inc.

"*The Leader's Voice* blew me away. It's just plain fun to read. Full of delightful stories, quirky facts, and inspiring imagery, I recommend this to every leader I know. It inspired me. At times, the book is even poetic. It's got an emotional intensity that's palpable. I laughed out loud and nodded my head in agreement. Clarke and Crossland offer an easy to understand and immediately applicable process for more persuasively communicating with your constituents. Do yourself a favor. Read this book."

—James M. Kouzes, Coauthor,
The Leadership Challenge and *Encouraging the Heart*

The Leader's Voice

THE
LEADER'S
VOICE

How your communication can inspire
action and get results!

CLARKE & CROSSLAND

select books

To Ruth and our four wonderful children, Jacqueline,
Shellie, Rob, and Scott.
— *Boyd Clarke*

To all the unsung and sung leaders, from the boiler room
to the boardroom, who spoke from their hearts
about work that matters.
— *Ron Crossland*

FOREWORD *BY TOM PETERS*

"Leadership is ultimately an act of faith in other people."
"Vision is a love affair with an idea."
"The aspiration to achieve something worthy or significant is common among the most common of people."

This really is a book about leading and leaders. Why start with that point? Because so many books on leadership turn me off, to be frank. They short-change the emotion, the passion, the care, the connection between leaders and followers. They apply reductionist B-school thinking to the one topic above all that is not amenable to reductionist thinking—leadership.

Nothing is more important than leadership—in general, and particularly in confusing times like these. And in my view, none have done a better job of getting at the True Essence of leading and leaders than my colleagues Boyd Clarke and Ron Crossland.

They are my colleagues, so this could be seen as a self-serving introduction. Problem is, I hold my closest friends to a much higher standard than others. I informed Boyd and Ron months ago that I would not write this foreword unless I "love the book" (I do. They passed. I'm writing). Moreover, I have the advantage of having observed the two of them, hands dirty, working with hundreds of client leaders on the slippery topic of leading—with peerless results. Which is to say that every idea in this book has successfully withstood the test of real folks—and very real feedback.

To "get" this book, you'll do no better than to reflect on the title: *The Leader's Voice.* Voice ... not plan or scheme. From the subtitle: "Communication." "Inspire Action." Leader. Voice. Inspiration. Action. Add in the words from the three quotes from the book that I opened with: "act of faith in other people"; "Vision ... love affair with an idea"; "aspiration to achieve something worthy or significant is common."

Last summer I was doing a minor bit of writing on leadership myself. I was highly dissatisfied with what I'd written. All of it seemed to add up to leaders doing something "to" people/followers. I came across a quote from my pal and management guru Karl Weick. Karl claimed that the three most important words in the leader's lexicon are "I don't know." That is, leaders don't "do things to" people/followers. Rather, they help people/followers find causes worth signing up for—and then the leaders and followers create totally unexpected adventures, far beyond each other's initial comprehension.

This is also the heart (right word!) of *THE LEADER'S VOICE*. Plans and execution thereof are obviously important—and the authors hardly shortchange that idea. But the paramount issue is a commitment to something worthy of followers' Emotional Investment. Another management expert I deeply respect, Richard Farson, made (in retrospect) an obvious assertion. He said that attempting to erase the pervasive organizational "fear of failure" was a useless waste of time. Fear of failure can be erased, he vowed, but only by one thing: getting people engaged in tasks and aims and visions worth taking heat for. Hey, why should I "risk it," if I am not totally turned on by the possible consequences of what I'm aiming to do?

Clarke and Crossland thus go on . . . and on . . . and on . . . about ideas such as authenticity. And the power of great (FROM THE HEART! DAMN IT!) storytelling. These ideas are . . . *THE LEADER'S VOICE*. These ideas are at the heart of creating . . . PASSIONATE ALIGNMENT.

Yes, Boyd and Ron: I LOVE THIS BOOK. The stories are inspiring. The ideas are time-tested. The ideas are not only "right on," but they fill a gaping void in the leadership literature. Plus, the timing is right. From the world of the corporation to the world of Washington D.C., understanding the true roots of leadership-that-moves-mountains (and gets your face on mountains, like Rushmore) has never (literally!) been more important.

In fact, I believe this book is a Rushmorean accomplishment—worthy of the deep contemplation of leaders and would-be leaders who are determined to Connect and Inspire . . . and Make a Difference.

Bravo!

West Tinmouth, VT
June 3, 2002

ACKNOWLEDGEMENTS

Writing can be solitary, but manufacturing a book takes a group effort. Talented individuals added their touch of genius to this work, and we thank them all for their contributions.

Geoff Thatcher aided us with stories, case studies, and focus. His bluntness was a whetstone of refinement, as he always challenged us to remain true to our thesis. We get attracted to scenic turnouts at times, and Geoff brought us back to the main journey. He worked with us late in the night, early in the morning, and at times throughout long days. A couple of times he multitasked, caring for his newborn while helping us rewrite.

Cheryl Boys quietly read through tangled masses of bad rough drafts, proofing our mistakes. Jill Hughes's expertise at copyediting and fact checking is a towering competence that makes us feel sloppy and unschooled by comparison. Ken Silvia makes music with images, text, and paper—an artistry beyond our expectations. Nancy Tansy chuckled the whole way through, helping us with countless odd jobs and bizarre requests. Kenzi Sugihara, our publisher, gently guided us through delays, setbacks, and missed deadlines. We hope his investment in us is repaid tenfold.

All writers have inspirational mentors. The late John W. Gardner was generous with time and attention for two unknown and somewhat naïve young men many years ago. We have never forgotten that he treated us like we counted. Our business partner, Tom Peters, is the Leonardo da Vinci of business communication. Always fresh, always communicating simultaneously at hefty decibels on the factual, emotional, and symbolic channels, he keeps us challenged and inspired. Jim Kouzes and Barry Posner have inspired us through their research and writing. We admire their dedication to "liberating the leader in everyone."

To our colleagues at tompeterscompany!, both in the United States and the United Kingdom, we find all expressions of gratitude inadequate. This band of renegade consultants, irrepressible sales folks, and untiring professional staff has applauded all the way through. We've never run a marathon, with cheering squads spaced along the track, but we know how runners feel at mile nineteen when a colleague hands off a cup of water and shouts, "You're doing great!"

Chuck Thompson, formerly director of worldwide sales for Motorola's semi-conductor business, challenged us for ten years by raising the bar each time he hired us. Chuck's faith in our abilities was always higher than our own. We must have hit his mark well enough or he'd have fired us.

Our friends and business partners at International Leadership Associates—Steve Houchin, Steve Coats, and Tom Heuer—encouraged us to get this book written during our working lifetimes. We thank them for many indulgences.

Accountants often retire unheralded. Over the years our business has been made stronger through the faithful attention of a consummate accounting professional, Randy Howard. Thanks for paying attention to our business like it was yours so that we could focus on customers and research.

And to Anne Carter we owe special thanks. Since she joined us she has made our customers feel special and has made us look better through her dedication to doing the right thing every time.

FIRST WORD

Renowned actor James Earl Jones has a powerful, penetrating, and memorable voice. From Darth Vader to "This is CNN," his voice is recognized throughout the world. In his autobiography, *James Earl Jones: Voices and Silences,* he writes about how his family moved from their sharecropper farm in Mississippi to Detroit when he was just six years old. This difficult transition triggered a stuttering crisis so profound that he hardly spoke a word for eight years.

In a high school English class, James Earl and his classmates were asked to write a poem and recite it before the class. He completed the first part of the assignment and received a challenging note from a determined but caring teacher, Donald Crouch: "I'm impressed with your poem, James Earl.... I know how hard it is for you to talk, and I don't require you to do that. Unfortunately, it is hard for me to know if these are your words. This is a fine poem. Did you copy it from somebody?'"

James Earl wrote about the incident. "My honor was at stake. Plagiarism was bad business. I had written every word of this poem myself.... I was shaking as I stood up, cursing myself. I strained to get the words out, pushing from the bottom of my soul. I opened my mouth—and to my astonishment, the words flowed out smoothly, every one of them." He wrote that his classmates were all amazed, "not so much by the poem as by the performance." In a single moment, James Earl Jones learned an important lesson about leadership communication.

Make sure the words are yours.

Push them from the very bottom of your soul.

The performance will take care of itself.

CONTENTS

The
Leader's
Voice

Chapter One

The biggest problem with leadership communication is
the illusion that it has occurred.

Just after World War II, a fifty-year-old Golda Meir came to the United States trying to raise funds for what would very soon be the state of Israel. For her, it was another challenge. This strong woman had been born into poverty in the Ukrainian capital of Kiev in 1898. After immigrating to the United States, she grew up and later taught school in Milwaukee. After marrying, Golda and her new husband moved to Palestine. From 1921 until the creation of Israel, Meir held key positions in the Jewish Agency, the highest Jewish authority in the British-controlled region.

Prior to Israel's historic declaration of independence, Golda had already fought a good fight. She had seen Palestine's Jewish population grow from about 65,000 to more than 800,000. She had experienced the Arab revolts of the late 1930s as Britain struggled to keep its conflicting commitments to both the Jews and Palestinians. Golda welcomed survivors of the Holocaust in the days following World War II. She helped lead her country in the civil war that erupted after the British left in 1947. She witnessed firsthand the political posturing and inefficiencies of the newly chartered United Nations. And she knew the fighting over Palestine would continue. Sadly, Golda was right.

At this pivotal moment, Israel desperately needed money. At the request of Jewish leader David Ben-Gurion, Golda went to the United States to raise the five million dollars essential to defend the Jews in Palestine against expected Arab attacks. However, upon arriving in January 1948, she was told by several prominent advisors that the American community had already given generously and would be hard-pressed to give more. American Jews, she was told, were tiring of hearing how badly money was needed.

It was in this context that Golda made an unscheduled appearance before the Council of Jewish Federations in Chicago. Our favorite interpretation of this true story is from Michael Avallone's novelization of *A Woman Called Golda*.

Golda had prepared no formal speech and was appearing before an audience who did not want to hear her message. However, she knew exactly what she wanted to say. Golda was prepared. For thirty years she had struggled to support the cause. Over this time she had matured from blind idealism to a strong but realistic worldview. She fiercely believed in her cause, and it was her beliefs and her honesty she relied upon. This is what she said:

> Please believe me when I tell you that I have not come to the United States only because several hundred thousand Jews are in danger of being killed. That is not the issue.
>
> The issue is that if the Jews of Palestine survive, then the Jews of the world survive with them, and their freedom will be assured forever. But if these several hundred thousand are wiped off the face of the earth, then there will be no Jewish people as such and for centuries to come, all our hopes and dreams of a Jewish nation, a Jewish homeland, will be smashed.
>
> My friends, when I say we need money immediately, I don't mean next week. I mean right now. In less than four months we will be fighting for our lives against cannon and armor. It is not for you to decide whether we will fight. That decision is taken: We will fight. We will pay for the birth of our nation with our blood. That is normal. The best among us will fall. That is certain. You can decide only one thing. Whether we win or we lose.

A long awkward silence was followed by thunderous applause and an avalanche of money. The odds against the Jews were overwhelming. They were surrounded. It was clear that the decision to fight had been made for them. Money was going to be essential for victory. These were the facts, plain and simple.

Freedom is often a blood-soaked ideal. Many would die, some horribly. Most American Jews had family and friends in Israel. Those who didn't certainly knew families who had relatives entwined in the conflict. It was personal. It was emotional.

The Jews had been hoping to restore their ancestral homeland for millennia. The horrors of the Holocaust fanned the fires of Zionism. The symbolic destiny of the Jews and Judaism was inseparably linked to the fate of the state of Israel.

After her speech and others like it, an anxious David Ben-Gurion called from Israel to ask Golda how much money she had raised. He was stunned. She had raised $50 million—ten times the amount Ben-Gurion had hoped.

On May 14, 1948, Israel declared independence. On May 15, Egypt, Syria, Lebanon, Jordan, and Iraq attacked. A long eight months later, the first Arab-Israeli War ended.

Ben-Gurion later said about Golda, "Someday when history will be written, it will be said that there was a Jewish woman who got the money which made the state possible." Golda Meir communicated with power. She laid out the facts to her audience, appealed to their emotions, and helped them understand the symbolic importance of Israel's existence. Her leadership made the seemingly impossible possible. Golda had the voice of a leader and the people did more than listen—they acted!

To be sure, there were other great things about her. However, this book is not about Golda Meir. It's not even about great world leaders. It's about *your* leadership, *your* voice. We could spend dozens of pages talking about John F. Kennedy's charisma, Margaret Thatcher's fortitude and Mahatma Gandhi's *satyagraha,* or "steadfastness in truth." Personally, we'd love to talk about Winston Churchill's perseverance, Martin Luther King's eloquence and Anwar Sadat's vision of peace. But this is a business book about leadership communication.

The Greek mathematician Archimedes discovered how to move the "whole earth." All he needed was a lever long enough and a place to stand. The task of uniting a business and moving it forward can feel as difficult. The ability to communicate powerfully is the leverage leaders need and most lack. The late John W. Gardner, an expert on public sector leadership, wrote, "Communication between leader and constituent is at the heart of everything." The heart of the matter for the business leader is to communicate so compellingly as to raise the consciousness, conviction, and competence of his or her constituency.

Most leaders, however, fail to create the organizational focus, commitment, and energy necessary to "move the whole organization." Over and over again business leaders make four fatal assumptions concerning their communication. These assumptions are:

1 Constituents UNDERSTAND what was communicated.
2 Constituents AGREE with what was communicated.
3 Constituents CARE about what was communicated.
4 Constituents will take APPROPRIATE ACTION.

The biggest problem with leadership communication is the illusion that it has occurred.

The principles outlined in this book *will* help you improve your communication, *but* we will not discuss mastering the *techniques* of communication. We have learned from sad experience that most leaders learn to communicate through imitating the techniques of others. While imitation may work as a starting place, it focuses too much on the surface displays of style and performance.

Imitation training focuses mostly on presentation and public speaking and teaches leaders to use strong gestures, a smile, good eye contact, and engaging stories. It tells them to speak with an active, lively language. Leaders are told to speak with a deep voice and talk to individuals, not the audience. They are commanded to never turn their back on the audience and to never, ever place their hands in their pockets. Above all, they must avoid the dreaded fig leaf maneuver. They are told, "Don't pace! Tell them what you are going to tell them, tell them and then tell them what you told them. Use humor sparingly, if at all." And that's just for oral presentations.

Written communication follows different rules and techniques. Most center on grammar, composition, and modern-day etiquette. Some e-mail letters read like assembly directions for a backyard swing set and others read like cryptic fortune cookies. Some corporate annual reports are stiffer than obituaries. Too many memos are indistinguishable from subpoenas. In fact, we have become painfully aware of the challenge involved in mastering written communication as we've written this book.

Imitation doesn't explore the deeper principles of communication but only polishes the surface. A few powerful principles will give you greater leverage than all the techniques you could learn in a lifetime of study. Beyond techniques, templates, and imitation lie the principles of "The Leader's Voice." When applied, they help leaders become more powerful and more influential. Principles trump techniques every time!

These principles are the lever, but like Archimedes, leaders also need a place to stand. When leaders know what they stand for and apply these principles, they can expect superior results.

Developing The Leader's Voice requires you to gain clarity and depth in the following areas:

Authenticity: Who am I as a leader? What motivates me to lead? Why have I taken up this mantle? What fears and aspirations drive me? What do I truly believe? Can I make a difference?

Foresight: What is our vision and/or brand identity? Where will our strategic direction ultimately lead us? How will my call for action be remembered over time? What kind of organization do we aspire to become and why?

Connection: How do I get through the fog? How do I create more meaningful conversations? How do I create greater alignment? How do I communicate with constituents publicly and privately?

Context: What is required of leaders now? What will success demand of us? What motivates associates? How will market forces, politics, and current trends impact my company?

Answer these questions, and you will have a place to stand. However, even when you stand for something, you still may not be able to communicate. As advisors, we have often found ourselves in the communication wasteland between business leaders and their constituents. Business leaders, strategically positioned in their command posts, know where they are, know who they want to communicate with, and know what they want to say. Unfortunately, the troops hunkered down in the trenches never "get" the message.

We have paid close attention to how business leaders attempt to communicate across this strangled divide, and we have gathered intelligence on the language that seems to make it through the fog of business.

The most effective communicators use three essential channels to convey important leadership messages and to overcome the four fatal assumptions. These channels are:

Factual

Emotional

Symbolic

Everyone uses these channels, but most have developed an overreliance upon one or two and allow the others to atrophy. This is like practicing only swimming when training for a triathlon.

An Orville Wright quote once graced the wall of the museum at the Wright Brothers National Memorial in Kitty Hawk, North Carolina: "Isn't it astonishing that all these secrets have been preserved for so many years just so that we could discover them?" In a small way we share this same feeling of amazement. The complex world of leadership communication became understandable as simple patterns emerged. Success became more predictable. When we coached others, their success surprised us. We hope that what we have discovered can help you and your organization fly.

Several years ago we were hired to consult with LensCrafters. This amazing company was founded and flourished because two entrepreneurs discovered a secret that had been preserved. As you probably know, before LensCrafters, buying a new pair of glasses involved going through your doctor and waiting several days or weeks for the prescription to be filled at a lab.

The secret was that it really took the labs only one hour to do the work. Seeing its potential, LensCrafters brought the lab to the people in 1983 when the first LensCrafters opened in Florence, Kentucky. Before long, there was a second store. The one-hour concept caught on quickly with busy consumers.

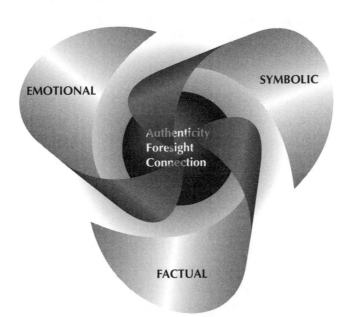

LensCrafters, from inception, was a company driven by an entrepreneur's dream and an innovator's heart. By the second year, dozens of locations were opened and the company had established its guiding vision and values. During the spring of 1986 two stores were opening per week, and by 1988, just five years after its inception, LensCrafters had 278 stores in the United States. It was an entrepreneur's dream come true.

However, like many companies with a soaring start, business began to plateau. Ban Hudson, LensCrafters' highly regarded leader during this first phase, moved to become CEO of U.S. Shoe, LensCrafters' parent company. Ban tapped Dave Browne to be his successor. A brash thirty-year-old executive, Browne was charged with taking LensCrafters to the next level.

For a company with such amazing success, this was no small task. Nevertheless, if anyone could do it, Dave Browne could. He was one of those unique individuals who glowed with success and confidence. He was brilliant when it came to financial analysis, retail operations, and marketplace leverage. Like an MBA on steroids, he brought the discipline of steel-trap analysis to a hard-working gang of passionate mavericks. He was competitive and needed to win. Dave was the kind of executive that Wall Street loves.

However, Dave was a self-proclaimed "numbers-only butthead." Dave's primary problem was that he relied too much on the factual channel. Those around him appreciated his genius and respected him, but it was clear that while he was the CEO and the boss, he was not the leader of the company. Unfortunately, he was suffering from one of those side effects that often come along with analytical brilliance: He was unable to inspire people to the next level because he was only dealing in facts. "I knew every detail," he said. He was trapped in the factual channel mantra of better, faster, cheaper.

While LensCrafters needed to look inward to improve efficiency and productivity, the company and Dave Browne were struggling to provide any reason beyond facts for associates to change. "I only talked about the head, never the heart," Dave told us. We watched as a gutsy company full of passion and pride began to look more like a best practices machine. While sales began to increase, passion and alignment began to fade. People made the numbers, but the numbers didn't stand for much besides scorekeeping.

We watched as Dave struggled to incorporate negative upward feedback. He began to feel the loss of company spirit he had enjoyed during Hudson's tenure and became personally concerned that maybe he had played a part in drowning the heart of an enterprise with data. Dave realized that he needed to change. "I needed to transform LensCrafters by transforming me." Wanting to rejuvenate the company's spirit, he pulled together a group of key LensCrafters associates to rework a vision to help celebrate their tenth anniversary. After much hard work, they announced the Decade II Vision, Mission and Core Values. The new vision was to "be the best at helping the world see." They wanted to be the "best" by "delivering legendary customer service" and by "developing and energizing associates and leaders in the world's best workplace." They also wanted to help the "world see by being conveniently available to people everywhere" and being the "first choice for eye care." However, the symbolic centerpiece of the vision was summed up in LensCrafters' promise of "giving the gift of sight to those who have the least and need us the most." In Dave's own words, "The Gift of Sight Program was the key to bringing more heart into the business."

While everyone knew Dave had approved the work that went into the vision and Gift of Sight program, no one really knew how deeply he cared about it until the day of the tenth-anniversary celebration in March 1993. A huge tent had been set up behind the headquarters building, where the typical corporate festivities were in swing. Dave took center stage to address his associates as he had many times before. But this day was different. He had ended his soul searching. To add to the emotion, LensCrafters had just passed Pearle Vision to become the largest optical retailer in the world, and an associate was critically ill in the hospital.

On this day, Dave did not stand and recite the numbers; he told a personal story. He recounted growing up on the streets of Philadelphia during some hard times. He let people know the principles his immigrant father, who was in the audience, had inspired. "My dad made sacrifices for me," he said, "He's been working as a mechanic at the same job his whole life." He told us that he was thinking about his faith and family and that he realized he didn't have to be the stereotypical "Wall Street CEO." Dave said, "I still wanted to win, I just wanted to win with heart." When he was finished speaking, he received a standing ovation. Not the obligatory applause of deference, but the applause of associates who were showing their appreciation for their leader as well as their boss.

> The genius of leadership is to speak with a voice that pushes past cynicism, doubt, and uncertainty.

As Dave Browne spread the news of the Decade II Vision, Mission and Core Values, he began to communicate the symbolism of the "gift of sight" with more emotion. His metaphor was simple: "Take the high ground before all others." He said the company was absolutely committed to treating everyone right. "We weren't going to cheat associates, bait and switch customers and sell through trivial promotions. We were going to take the high ground." And though the symbol was simple, the emotions were genuine. The people at LensCrafters began to feel the change.

The Gift of Sight program was especially important to Dave. He is quick to note that all of the work was done by the associates and others on his management team. "I said 'yes' and got out of the way." Today, the program has served more than two million underprivileged people in the United States and twenty-five developing countries around the world.

Once Dave Browne started communicating with facts, emotions, and symbols, LensCrafters left the plateau. It has become one of the greatest niche retail success stories ever. Dave did not stop being the MBA on steroids. He simply added the emotional and symbolic channels to his fact-based communication repertoire.

While we like to tell inspiring stories and reference Kennedy, King, Gandhi, and CEOs to make a point, we understand that most of the people in this world have regular jobs.

> "I'm not Golda Meir, Kennedy, or King. Never will be!"

> "I'm the struggling administrative coordinator, and what I do has no influence on whether my company will succeed or fail!"

> "I'm the Chief Operating Officer, and there's no way some vision thing will get my company to the next level."

If you are reading this book, you're a sales manager, a project director, an IT manager, a manufacturing supervisor, or a vice president. Who knows? You might even be a CEO.

Your company probably doesn't sell anything that will bring world peace. You aren't about to help found a nation or lead soldiers into battle. The products or services you sell might even be as ordinary as toilet bowl plungers or consulting. However, many of you are still dreamers, hoping that one day you might change the world. We all want to make a difference.

The Language of Followers

Spanish caballeros like Martín Hardoy have tried to understand *el lenguaje del caballo,* the language of horses. In the United States, Frank Bell, Ray Hunt, Buck Brannaman, and Monty Roberts, "The Man Who Listens To Horses," have taught us the words.

Traditional horse breaking requires the strenuous efforts of four or five people over many hours, sometimes days. There's a reason they call it *breaking*. It is violent. During the breaking there is yelling, whipping, and force but no communication. These new horse communicators have a different method and a different philosophy. Hardoy says, "The idea is to know how the horse thinks." Others call it "starting a horse." The technique uses communication to build a relationship. The language is the language of the horse, not the trainer. Its purpose is to ask the horse to join willingly.

We believe this communication process parallels the principles of effective leadership communication. To understand it better, we called Monty Roberts. While Monty is not without his critics, he is passionate about his beliefs. He talked to us about his philosophy and how it evolved over the years. As we watched one of his videos, we were amazed at how he stands eye-to-eye with the horse in a thirty-foot-square corral and communicates.

> A look in the eye, Roberts explains, means "go away from me." The horse moves to the other side of the corral. He moves a horse around the edge of the corral by gently tossing a cotton rope at the horse's hindquarters. The horse trots in a circle and begins to lick and chew. This means, "I am not afraid of you." The chase continues until the horse jerks its nose up and to the side. This means, "Let's not do this." Soon it drops its head, signaling, "I no longer want to flee."
>
> Monty stops the chase and stands with his back to the horse, a sign of trust and an invitation. Amazingly, the horse begins to approach. He turns and the horse follows. Oral reinforcement and gentle patting follow. Again he turns his back, walks, and again the horse joins him. Trust and connection replace rope and technique. Within minutes the horse nervously accepts a saddle. After feeling the saddle for a while and receiving more reassurance, the horse is finally ready for a rider. When the process is complete, this formerly wild horse nuzzles Monty's head and shoulder as if he were part of the herd.

Monty's method is so effective that Queen Elizabeth II invited him to England, where he started sixteen horses for the royal stables. As his phenomenal British success became publicized, he sold millions of books, appeared on *Oprah,* and ABC's *Nightline* aired his story.

These "horse whisperers" connect to horses by speaking the animals' language. The horses follow willingly, with energy and their spirits intact. On the other hand, broken horses comply with commands. While they work well, their spirits often seem diminished.

The same is true in business. The leader speaks. His followers applaud on command. There is an illusion that communication took place, but it didn't. Unfortunately, this communication failure breeds additional communication static. Over time, leaders resort to commands rather than communication. This leads to *breaking* talent, not *starting* it.

The Leader's Voice is the language of your associates, your constituents. They listen in facts, emotions, and symbols.

One Voice

We believe that one voice can make all the difference. One voice will be heard above the clamor of the crowd, above the noise of the street, and above the stampede in the market. When we hear it, we respond. It resonates with our best intentions and aspirations. Like the bellows of a blacksmith, it fans the flames of desire to rise above the mundane and make a mark. It encourages us to do great work, to be extraordinary. It energizes and unites.

It is The Leader's Voice.

This one voice simplifies the complex and clarifies the cloudy. It quiets dissonance and strikes the chord that defines direction. It replaces despair with hope and cynicism with purpose. It plainly states the unspoken, describes precisely what people feel but fear to say, and calls others to action when they are paralyzed. The genius of leadership is to speak with a voice that pushes past cynicism, doubt, and uncertainty.

The Leader's Voice allows you to speak the truth so others can distinguish it from spin. It establishes a compelling context, while others squabble over trivial content. It challenges others to take a stand, before certainty arrives. It is authentically your voice. Even when your words feel clumsy, your voice is eloquent. When your passion declares the direction you will go, it unites those who would follow and divides those who will not.

If you choose to lead, prepare to take a stand. It is not for the fainthearted. Some will judge you unfairly, blaming you for their lack of success. Others will expect resources you cannot give, answers that you do not have, and permission you cannot grant. You will be misquoted. Your judgment will be questioned.

You will certainly stumble. Failure will stalk you like a predator. Do you think Golda Meir and Dave Browne failed? Of course they did—sometimes spectacularly. The toughest problems will be yours alone. You must take responsibility for the failures and give credit for the successes. Lose the fantasy that you will be cherished, immortalized, and revered. Expect long hours and few moments of gratitude.

Expect also that some will soar beyond your expectations. They will create magic inspired by your dream. They will make you glad you chose to lead. They will hear what you say, understand it, care about it, and act. Together, you will engage in the best work of your lives.

Please join us in a conversation about how to improve your business leadership communication. Add your voice at **www.theleadersvoice.biz**. Books often portend finality, while Web sites promise renewal. We offer both. Truth is, we love to explore and create. Talk to us. Challenge us. Teach us.

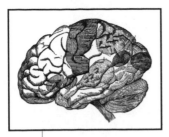

Hardwired
For Facts,
Emotions
& Symbols

Chapter Two

Reason without emotion is **impossible.**

Aristotle studied under Plato and tutored Alexander the Great. While modern discoveries have replaced his natural science observations, his work on rhetoric—the art of persuasion and poetry—has guided communication theory for more than two thousand years. Aristotle described three kinds of persuasive oratory. The forensic is intended to prove—FACTS. The deliberative is intended to move or restrain an audience—EMOTIONS. And the ceremonial is intended to display sentiments—SYMBOLS. While Aristotle mistakenly thought the brain functioned like a car's radiator, cooling the blood to prevent the heart from overheating, his communication observations hit dead center. His genius is further revealed when viewed in the light of modern neurological science.

Over the past decade, scientists have learned more about the human brain than during the prior two centuries. The brain is comprised of more than a dozen complex organs working in conjunction to produce memory and reason, provide consciousness, and regulate the body. From a communications perspective, the human brain is engineered to send, receive, and evaluate using facts, emotions, and symbols. Left brain/right brain models or even the Triune brain model have been replaced with a more complete picture of this complex system of organs.

For many years we knew that communicating in facts, emotions, and symbols worked, but we didn't always completely understand why. It was only after studying neurology that we understood the brain's role in communication. It is vital to understand that the human brain is hardwired to

think in facts, emotions, and symbols. To speak with The Leader's Voice is to speak as the brain works.

The Phineas Effect

Phineas P. Gage had a mind-altering experience in 1848. A dynamic, young construction foreman for the Rutland & Burlington Railroad, he was admired by his colleagues and respected by his crew. He worked tirelessly and thoughtfully at a demanding job.

Gage and his gang were clearing the right-of-way along the Black River near the town of Cavendish, Vermont. Taking responsibility for one of the more dangerous tasks, Phineas prepared blasting holes for detonation by tamping gunpowder into holes with a specially designed iron rod. It was a task that required concentration and precision.

One day, Phineas slipped.

His rod ignited the powder and the explosion rocketed the iron rod through his left cheek, his left eye, and the top of his head. The rod whistled through the air and landed dozens of yards away. Thrown to the ground by the blast, the young man sat stunned and silent but fully awake. His men immediately rushed him to the local town doctor, who was amazed to see the railroad foreman alive. Gage suffered a mild infection, some mild fevers, and lost his left eye. Within two months he was released from the doctor's care.

It was a miracle.

Gage, still physically robust, seemed able to communicate fully. He was tested and shown to suffer no memory loss. His logical processes were intact. However, it soon became evident that his personality had permanently changed. He became fitful, irreverent, profane, impatient, obstinate, and indifferent to his fellow human beings. He became stuck in a cycle of flitting from one plan to another, never following through. His emotional energy was high, untamed, and often uncontrolled. His behavior changed so radically that some former friends had trouble even recognizing him. Though still physically competent, the railroad let him go due to his dramatic character change. Friends who knew the "before" and "after" Phineas said, "Gage was no longer Gage." From gaucho, to stagecoach driver, to circus freak, he held many jobs, holding none of them long. At the age of thirty-eight, he lapsed into a coma and died.

The experience of Phineas Gage launched the modern era of brain research. His accident provided great insight into how the brain works. For example, doctors learned that his behavior change was due to losing a critical portion of his logical brain. In other words, when the logical no longer communicated with the emotional brain, not only does behavior change, but the ability to make decisions is severely degraded. The story of Phineas Gage, along with decades of other scientific studies and exacting work, has led scientists to several fundamental conclusions.

> By not using facts, emotions, and symbols in their communication, leaders leave out essential ingredients that stimulate and promote the transfer of meaning and quality decision making.

"Reason, without emotion, is neurologically impossible," states Antonio Damasio, a leading neurologist who has helped many nonscientists understand the brain through his accessible writing. Steven Pinker, the energetic director of MIT's Center for Cognitive Neuroscience, concurs with Damasio: "Emotions are adaptations, well-engineered software modules that work in harmony with the intellect and are indispensable to the functioning of the whole mind."

Like reason, decision making without emotion is neurologically impossible. Combined with additional brain research, we have concluded that leadership communication that minimizes facts or emotions degrades the quality of communication and subsequent decision making. For example, have you ever known someone who seems to run on pure logic or pure emotion? Have you ever made a decision while blind with anger? Have you ever made a decision while "stupid in love?" Have you ever made a decision with your head that your heart knew was wrong? Our technical term for folks like this is "messed up." No one runs on total facts or total emotion. These parts of the brain are hardwired together.

Communication Lobotomy

A medical lobotomy, as practiced in the 1950s, involved inserting an ice pick over the eyeball and piercing the orbit right down into the frontal lobes of the brain. Once there, the doctors would destroy a portion of the brain. To save money, these caring doctors used electroshock therapy instead of anesthesia to dull the pain. Unfortunately, the ice pick had the nasty habit of sometimes breaking off in mid-surgery. To avoid the emergency operation required to remove the broken pick, doctors invented a strong and sharp steel rod that could penetrate the brain without breaking.

That sounds better, doesn't it?

The lobotomy was a radical treatment for mental illnesses such as schizophrenia or other situations in which patients were wildly emotional and unable to control their behavior. While the hysteria or wild behavior was relieved, the lobotomy produced an unintended effect. It reduced, or in some cases eliminated, the patient's ability to make simple decisions. It left many looking like Jack Nicholson at the end of *One Flew over the Cuckoo's Nest*. The sufferer had minimal emotional reaction to life. The effects in some cases

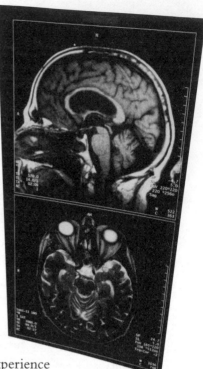

were so profound that some patients could experience intense hunger and articulate their need for food, but remain unable to make the decision to eat.

The emotional and logical parts of the brain also work with other neurological components, such as the somatic sensory system, to produce symbols. This is a complex process. A communication lobotomy minimizes a transfer of meaning, knowledge, and intent when it disrupts the brain's ability to integrate all three channels. By not using facts, emotions, and symbols in their communication, leaders leave out essential ingredients that stimulate and promote the transfer of meaning and quality decision making. All the facts in the world falling from the well-intentioned but emotionless lips of executives cannot reverse the condition. A communication lobotomy can turn normal, hard-working, motivated associates into fitful, irreverent, profane, impatient, obstinate, and indifferent ones. It stimulates cynicism as it chokes the life out of the symbols we cherish.

Yet, too many managers use verbal ice picks on their associates. Sometimes, just as in the real surgery, a broken piece of the ice pick is left embedded in the worker's psyche. These leaders are like Nurse Ratched with an MBA, ready to destroy any employee within the organization. While that may seem a little harsh, it's something that happens in big and small companies every day. This dysfunction leaves workers disconnected, discontented, and disengaged.

The following data should at least upset you and, more likely, shake you to your core. *Gallup Management Journal's* second annual nationwide 2001 employee engagement survey found that 55 percent were "not engaged."

Whoa . . . well, at least that leaves 45 percent who *were* engaged, right? No, it gets worse. Of the 1,001 working adults surveyed, another 19 percent were "actively disengaged." Gallup describes these individuals as workplace poison, suggesting that we would be better off if they didn't show up. While women were more engaged than men, and associates of smaller companies were more engaged than their counterparts at big companies, only 26 percent of the total sample were "engaged."

In telephone interviews, disengagement was measured by asking respondents, among other things, if they would recommend the company or its products, if they believed they were working at full potential, and if they planned to be with the company in the future. Initially, we wanted to reject the Gallup survey results as obviously overstated and completely ridiculous. It couldn't be that bad! After reviewing their research methods and measurement criteria, sadly, reluctantly, we came to believe.

While this is obviously a complex, multifaceted issue, communication is the primary way leaders create engagement. Every day leaders try to engage constituents in visions, missions, strategies, values, objectives, and goals through communication. If Gallup is right, most employees remain disengaged. As previously noted, we believe the number one problem with leadership communication is the illusion that it has actually occurred. Leaders habitually succumb to the sin of the four fatal assumptions. This communication illusion leaves leaders and constituents blaming each other.

At tompeterscompany!, our 2002 survey of 1,104 business professionals confirmed, yet again, the communication culprit. The professionals believe that 86 percent of their executives *feel* they are great communicators. However, only 17 percent believe their executives are, indeed, effective communicators. Additional data from Gallup's *First, Break All the Rules* shows that 71 percent of workers cited difficulties with their supervisor as their primary reason for leaving their most recent position. In 2001, Sterling, Virginia's, Supplee Group surveyed 2,000 former international employees who resigned from seven technology and professional service firms. Interviews revealed that not only was the boss the main reason people quit, but also that the boss's chief deficiency was "poor communication."

Unfortunately this data is no news flash. Periodically we have looked at the correlation between the disengaged worker and the communication ability of leaders. Our first indication that the leadership communication gap was actually a chasm occurred way back in 1986. In a report titled "Strategic Vision," Lou Harris and Associates and the *Los Angeles Times Mirror* shared the results of detailed interviews with 246 senior executives from America's largest companies. Each executive was asked to evaluate how effective he or she was at communicating the vision to the organization. Here were the results:

Very effective	47 percent
Somewhat effective	46 percent
Not too effective	4 percent
Not effective at all	1 percent
Not sure	2 percent

We continued the research by interviewing frontline managers and supervisors from many of the same companies, asking, "How effective are your senior executives at communicating the company's vision?" Survey says:

Very effective	8 percent
Somewhat effective	21 percent
Not too effective	32 percent
Not effective at all	38 percent
Not sure	1 percent

In 1989, organizational psychologist Philip H. Mirvis and Professor Donald L. Kanter published *The Cynical Americans: Living and Working in an Age of Discontent and Disillusion.* In their national survey of 649 workers, they classified 43 percent of workers and 40 percent of managers and supervisors as being cynical. They defined 14 percent as wary and only 38 percent as upbeat. They later reported that cynicism had risen from 43 percent to 48 percent by the mid-1990s.

The situation has gone from bad to worse over the last fifteen years. There are too many employees like Henry Flower. A talented designer, Henry was asked to revise his bio by his current employer's marketing director. While we've changed Henry's name and company to protect the innocent (and his job), this is what he wrote. And, yes, this is real:

Disengaging Henry

Henry Flower is a graduate of Cleveland Institute of Art with a Bachelor's of Fine Arts in Interior Design. Upon graduation Henry worked for Retail Forum Associates, RFA, in Columbus, Ohio. There he earned the nicknames of tiger, champ, ace, chief, and blood, and began his long string of working for bosses who couldn't remember his name.

After realizing that he'd been getting abused for the last three years in terms of overtime hours and any sense of compensation, he made the move to what he thought would be the plush, cushy world of corporate life. Thus began his career at AT&T GIS. It was a heady and glorious world of endless acronyms, senseless rules, regulations, and lack of accountability at all levels. Eventually the company was spun off and became its old self, NCR. All the dysfunctional systems were retained to make sure that NCR could be as inefficient and nonresponsive to clients as its predecessor. Finally, Henry decided maybe he should see if somebody needed a beaten-down, reamed-out sketch boy to help with a bottom line somewhere. It was at this point in January of 1998 that Henry made the jump to Fred Jenkins Design. The rest, as we say, is journeyman mediocrity.

Henry often maintains his creative spark by the extensive and frequent use of cannabis sativa. Also known by its other names, such as pot, cheeba, ganja, weed, Mary Jane, broccoli, sticky green, but it will always be marijuana to him. Henry furthers this spark through his various community outreach efforts, and his constant support of local food suppliers such as Burger King whenever a post-high munchies craze hits.

Henry continues to work on many projects, but after a while they all sort of run together into one mass of soul crushing, dispiriting dead ends, making him realize he should have gotten that accounting degree after all.

True story! Actual bio! And, he turned it in. The marketing director made some extensive revisions and Henry is still toiling away today. Our advice to Henry and his disengaged compatriots is to quit. Quit blaming others for the meaninglessness of your work. We also advise inept, inarticulate, and insipid leaders to accept responsibility for their failure to engage talented constituents who long to do great work.

How the hell did things get so bad? The answer goes beyond just communication and involves complex social forces at work.

The following two stories illustrate how poor communication contributes to disengagement.

Filling in the Blanks

Scene 1: The meeting starts with some initial fanfare, stirring music, a brief welcome, and then a key executive is introduced amid applause. She tells a good joke, and once the laughter subsides, the lights dim, the projectors beam, and you settle back for another mesmerizing PowerPoint presentation. She shows the company's vision for the coming year. However, instead of focusing on the speaker, you become almost hypnotized by the illuminated dark blue or purple hues and yellowish fonts on the projection screen.

It's not just the barrage of multicolored charts, graphs, and statistics swarming with facts that produce the slumber in your eyes. It's also the carefully scripted words of a person being politically correct, legally sanitized, and emotionally flat. You realize that she, or her assistant, has worked harder on the slides than on the message. New to the bells and whistles of PowerPoint, she uses the presupplied cash register sound to emphasize EBITDA, hoping technology will spur the enthusiasm she cannot. Result: another candidate for the PowerPoint Hall of Shame.

When it is over, you resign yourself to just reading the handout, three slides per page with no notes. During the awkward silence following the speaker's request for questions, you realize you do have questions but don't care enough to ask them. Most befuddling of all, you still are not clear about the message. You remember the vision statement, but you don't know the vision. You remember the facts, but you are fuzzy about the company's goals. The leader concludes to polite applause and during the subsequent cocktail hour receives the obligatory confirmation that it was the best presentation she ever made.

The problem is . . . it actually was.

Scene 2: The auditorium lights dim to the stirring sounds of Olympic trumpets. The inspirational video begins, highlighting the accomplishments of humankind and your division. You are feeling positive, uplifted, and even the most cynical in the audience feel proud. The executive takes the stage to loud applause. This time there are no slides and no notes. He talks in a dynamic, sincere voice, telling the inspiring story of the salesperson who went above and beyond to land the huge account. He describes in humorous detail what the vice president of international development had to eat while striking a new business deal in China.

The entertainment value is high, but the content value is low. You leave feeling alert and excited, but you still don't know what vital action to take for your company. You can sing the company's anthem and even like the tune. But once again, you don't really know the vision.

Both leaders fail because we process information using facts, emotions, and symbols. Detailed data alone works like chloroform. Scintillating stories alone work like nitrous oxide. When leaders communicate facts alone, constituents fill in the emotional and symbolic blanks. The same is true of the other channels. We always fill in the blanks. Remember, your brain works this way. When constituents fill in the blanks left by leaders, they construct a different message than the leader sent. Leaders, believing they have communicated completely, now fall into the fatal assumptions trap. What results is one of four things: a lack of understanding, a lack of agreement, a lack of caring, or a lack of appropriate action.

> **Detailed data alone works like chloroform. Titillating stories alone work like nitrous oxide.**

We began our pursuit years ago as amateur organizational anthropologists curious about why some leaders are naturally great communicators. As entrepreneurs we thought teaching leaders how to communicate more effectively could be an interesting way to make a buck or two. After learning what worked, we were compelled to learn *why* it worked. This chapter has been about the *why*.

Demosthenes was a great orator during Greece's Golden Age. He was no natural genius at the art. His first speeches were embarrassing, miserable failures. In order to perfect his art, he shaved half his head and retreated to a cave.

During his day, a half-shaved head was a public no-no. He quarantined him-self in order to reflect on what he most desperately had to say. He labored to find his passion, his sense of identity, and his reason to communicate. He thought about what his Greek constituency truly valued and the language that most spoke to them.

Then Demosthenes practiced speaking from his heart. When he emerged he won the admiration of the toughest critics the world has ever known. His name has been married to eloquence for more than two thousand years.

So keep reading or go shave your head.

PROD. NO. *drama*
SCENE TAKE ROLL
DATE SOUND
PROD. CO.
DIRECTOR
CAMERAMAN

How TNT Found Drama

Chapter Three

TNT needed to position itself as 100 percent dramatic entertainment that makes you think and feel.

T NT is one of cable television's great success stories. Created and launched by Ted Turner in 1988, it grew from an audience of seventeen million to more than fifty million in less than two years. In the early days, the Atlanta-based TNT was known for its Westerns and classic movies, which the network leveraged from the MGM film library that Turner had purchased.

As the network grew, it added World Championship Wrestling, NFL, NBA, and the Winter Olympics. Production of original movies became a centerpiece of its programming. Historical dramas such as *Gettysburg, Andersonville,* and *George Wallace* earned big ratings and were praised by critics. Throughout the 1990s, TNT consistently delivered some of cable's highest ratings. In 1996, TNT ranked number one in prime time thanks to the power of the NFL, NBA, and WCW and scored four of the top ten highest-rated movies on basic cable. Advertised as the "best movie studio on television," the network defined itself internally with an understood positioning:

"TNT is for upscale adult couples and families looking for quality-driven television. TNT is the premiere basic cable network offering a variety of blue-chip sports and entertainment programs."

TNT continued to dominate through its ten-year anniversary in 1998. NASCAR, PGA, and Wimbledon were acquired. Tiger Woods, Venus Williams, John Stockton, and others could be seen on the network. TNT's original movies earned big numbers, rave reviews, and attracted marquee Hollywood stars. In 1999, TNT captured four of the top five highest-rated

Pictured left, Alec Baldwin starred in the TNT Original film "Nuremberg."

original movies on basic cable. In 2000, TNT's *Nuremberg* and *Running Mates* tied as the highest-rated original movies.

TNT was in more than eighty million homes, which is 97 percent of American homes with cable or satellite television. In other words, if you get cable, you get TNT. The network reaped substantial profits from both cable subscriptions and advertising.

Despite all its great success, TNT's executives knew they had to change— and fast. As cable television proliferated from a handful of channels in 1988 to hundreds in the year 2000, TNT was finding itself positioned as a general variety network with diminishing brand power. TNT broadcast everything from Hulk Hogan smashing bodies on WCW to Juliette Binoche falling in love in *The English Patient*. The network's marketers and programmers struggled to find focus amid the variety. "In the TV business, focus was the f-word," said Scot Safon, TNT's senior vice president of marketing. "It meant you'd be deliberately limiting your appeal."

Ratings were still strong, but viewers didn't know what to expect. However, viewers identified with the brands of Lifetime (women), ESPN (sports), MTV (music), and TNT's competitors. A few crude scribbles drawn by adult viewers at research focus groups confirmed the executives' worst fears: TNT stood for everything, instead of something.

Pencil Drawings from TNT Focus Groups

"Viewers don't know what to expect from TNT."

As the network's executive vice president and general manager, Steve Koonin, put it, "We were known for our parts while other networks were known for the sum of their parts." TNT lacked distinction in the new television world of two hundred brands. YES, two hundred television brands, all vying for your eyeballs, your loyalty, your time, and advertisers' dollars!

Bradley J. Siegel, who oversees all of Turner Broadcasting's entertainment networks, hired Koonin in February 2000 to lead TNT's brand initiative. Siegel had been friends with Koonin for a few years and had admired his work at Coca-Cola. Known for his robust humor and love for alliteration, Koonin immediately touted his "three P's": "We needed to POSITION the network, PROGRAM to the positioning, and then PROMOTE the programming and positioning," he said.

As the leader, Koonin had to turn a big billion-dollar ship during a "perfect storm." TNT was launching its first ever brand initiative during the worst media market in a lifetime. At the same time, TNT and Turner Broadcasting were being merged along with the rest of Time Warner into AOL. Ad sales were down, budgets were being cut, and layoffs were required. For a few months in early 2001, nervous questions swirled through the hallways of TNT headquarters at 1050 Techwood Drive. "Has your project been killed?" "Did you hear so-and-so was let go?" "Are we moving our offices to New York?" AND . . . the entire senior level executive team at Turner Broadcasting was shuffled right in the middle of the brand initiative.

So, to chart this course, Koonin assembled a fantastic team of people around him. They were, to name a few, Scot Safon in marketing, Jennifer Dorian on branding, Karen Cassell managing public relations, Jon Marks conducting the research, Michael Borza and Ron Korb handling the on-air creative, and Ken Schwab in programming.

The TNT team did their research, analyzed the competition, and listened to their customers and associates. They formulated hypothetical brand positionings reflecting TNT's heritage. They became experts in such things as the traits of a "broadcast couch potato" vs. "highbrows." They rigorously studied network attributes, perceptual maps, and viewer segmentation studies.

During the research phase of the brand initiative, Koonin and his team took the unusual and welcome step of involving the entire staff. "We shared research with everyone," he said, "but we made it easy to understand."

Over the course of a few months, the facts began to reveal the new positioning for the network. Since the research was being shared, it was clear for everyone to see that TNT needed to position itself as "100 percent dramatic entertainment that makes you think and feel." The first working term uncovered was "the drama club." It represented both TNT's strongest audience and its best prospects for growth.

There is always a vulnerable moment just after the facts are communicated when people interpret the facts through their own emotional and symbolic filters. At TNT, it came in the form of questions and concerns: "What if drama is boring?" "Is drama too limiting?" "Drama can be really highbrow." "Drama is so *Masterpiece Theater*." "Hey, we're not PBS!"

Leaving constituents with just the facts is a recipe for disaster. Koonin could have assumed that associates UNDERSTOOD the facts the same way he did, AGREED with his interpretation of the facts, CARED about what he cared about, and would take ACTION similar to his. However, without saying it in so many words, Steve Koonin believes in the principles of The Leader's Voice. While we call it facts, emotions, and symbols, he calls it "research," "fun," "humor," "vision," and "repetition."

In order to put their own emotional and symbolic stamp on "the drama club," TNT organized a corporate retreat for two hundred associates and executives at the Boca Raton Resort and Club in Florida on September 27,

"Meat and Potatoes" Growth Strategy

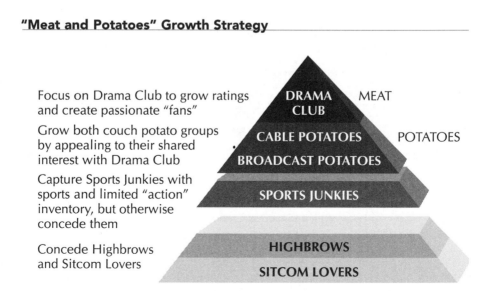

Focus on Drama Club to grow ratings and create passionate "fans"

Grow both couch potato groups by appealing to their shared interest with Drama Club

Capture Sports Junkies with sports and limited "action" inventory, but otherwise concede them

Concede Highbrows and Sitcom Lovers

DRAMA CLUB — MEAT

CABLE POTATOES / BROADCAST POTATOES — POTATOES

SPORTS JUNKIES

HIGHBROWS

SITCOM LOVERS

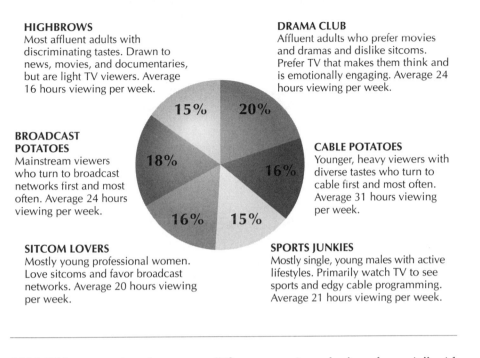

HIGHBROWS
Most affluent adults with discriminating tastes. Drawn to news, movies, and documentaries, but are light TV viewers. Average 16 hours viewing per week.

DRAMA CLUB
Affluent adults who prefer movies and dramas and dislike sitcoms. Prefer TV that makes them think and is emotionally engaging. Average 24 hours viewing per week.

BROADCAST POTATOES
Mainstream viewers who turn to broadcast networks first and most often. Average 24 hours viewing per week.

CABLE POTATOES
Younger, heavy viewers with diverse tastes who turn to cable first and most often. Average 31 hours viewing per week.

SITCOM LOVERS
Mostly young professional women. Love sitcoms and favor broadcast networks. Average 20 hours viewing per week.

SPORTS JUNKIES
Mostly single, young males with active lifestyles. Primarily watch TV to see sports and edgy cable programming. Average 21 hours viewing per week.

2000. This was a pivotal moment. "If your associates don't embrace it," said TNT's branding guru, Jennifer Dorian, "you have to trash it!"

To help them communicate and introduce the brand identity, Koonin hired conductor Boris Brott. Their goal was to communicate through music the importance of playing together. With the respect and authority that only a maestro can command, Brott told the associates, "Only with the same song sheet can we perform in harmony." Using Beethoven's struggle for perfection as a business metaphor, he related Ludwig's career, played his music, and then taught the entire staff of TNT to play "Ode to Joy" with tone bars, a device like a one-note xylophone.

Can you hear the beauty of two hundred people learning to play the same song, with harmony, in one short session? "It was an exciting and unifying moment," Koonin said. The meeting ended with TNT's leaders handing out sheet music inked with TNT's new brand positioning and defining the elements of drama. Every employee returned to the network's Atlanta headquarters knowing what brand tune they had to play. The message was powerful and clear. "I am the conductor," Koonin said, "and we all need to play off the same song sheet." Listed on the song sheet were attributes to help associates find the drama that "makes you think and feel."

TNT Personality

TNT is not:	TNT is:	TNT is not:
Juvenile	Contemporary	Old-fashioned
Mindless	Meaningful	Elitist
Predictable	Suspenseful	Dull
Frivolous	Exciting	Slow
Superficial	Powerful	Self-important

This retreat in Florida was held nearly ten months before TNT launched its new brand. This was before TNT had a tagline, new logo, or a new advertising campaign. People aligned with the emerging brand because Koonin communicated factually, emotionally, and symbolically. Passionately aligned, everyone worked the next ten months back in Atlanta preparing for the brand launch despite budget cuts, layoffs, and a terrible ad market. Ideas percolated, decisions were made, and creative plans came alive.

Oh, don't you wish it were so easy?

Wrestling With WrestleMania

The network's top-rated show was *WCW Monday Nitro,* which frequently held the number one position as the week's highest-rated program on basic cable. Produced by Turner Broadcasting's World Championship Wrestling, the show was a spectacle of hard bodies, screaming fans, bikini-clad dancers, and fireworks. Wrestling was a juvenile, frivolous, mindless, and sweaty 240-pound muscle-bound symbol of everything the network was not going to be. AND EVERYONE KNEW IT!

Scot Safon was a big fan of the new brand positioning, but he expressed what others felt. "The notion that we can be a drama brand while still keeping WCW on the schedule is, well, I mean, who are we kidding?" An industry veteran, he knew that networks just don't cancel their top-rated show.

TNT did.

Scot had a conversion moment. "That was our top-rated show by more than double anything else, and we dumped it! Can you name another network that cancelled its top-rated show? I don't know if consumers noticed that we dropped wrestling from our schedule, but it said *everything* to the staff."

Tuesday, June 12, 2001, was chosen as brand launch day. Everyone gathered in one of Turner's cavernous studios for D-Day (Drama Day). TNT's new logo and tagline were unveiled to America. Following the live on-air introduction of the new logo, a three-minute advertisement called "What is drama?" premiered. It showcased Whoopi Goldberg, Dennis Hopper, Joan Allen, and other Hollywood stars celebrating drama. The message was clear, simple, and impossible to miss: "TNT. We Know Drama."

That night kicked off TNT's new programming, on-air packaging, and a three-month media plan to tout TNT's new brand promise as a destination for dramatic entertainment. By their one-year anniversary, the results were astounding. TNT became cable's number one destination for drama and has seen double-digit growth in key demographics. TNT grew 50 percent among adults 18 to 49 with household incomes of $75,000 plus. As you can imagine, this demographic is gold to advertisers. Because of its strong line-up of dramatic movies, TNT has become the most-watched and highest-rated basic cable network in weekend prime time for not only the 18- to 49-year-olds, but also viewers 18 to 34 and 25 to 54.

Just as he had done in preparing for the launch, Koonin continued to communicate with The Leader's Voice. He delivered facts, ratings, ad sales, and other information to the associates on a regular basis. "We are lucky," he said, "to be in a business where we get a report card every day."

Its programming department, focused by the new brand, has acquired dramas like *NYPD Blue, X-Files, Judging Amy, Law & Order,* and *ER* and movies like *Erin Brockovich* and *The Perfect Storm.*

Creativity exploded across the network as associates embraced the new brand. "For us," Koonin said, "branding went from a buzz word to a lifestyle." This lifestyle includes a variety of activities. Inspired by their "What is drama?" advertising spots, TNT's on-air department created internal spots showcasing associates talking about "what is dramatic about working at TNT." The answers ranged from "finding a parking space" to "working with great people."

Drama was in the hallways and in the work. "Morale is high and even our meetings have become dramatic," he said. One of the brand's best measures of success is the associate backlash Koonin gets when intentionally suggesting something that's "off brand."

"We had a competition in our on-air department to identify the attributes of drama," Koonin said. Victory in the competition earned the person behind the winning idea a chance to produce a commercial featuring the attribute. Several great ideas were generated, from the drama of eating to the drama of flying. However, the winning idea featured the drama of crying.

Kleenex signed on immediately to sponsor a weekly "tear jerker" movie on TNT.

Other advertisers lined up. Johnson & Johnson collaborated with TNT to create a series of original television movies that celebrate the triumph of the human spirit. Hollywood movie studios paid TNT to attach stars such as Meg Ryan, Hugh Jackman, and Denzel Washington to the "What is drama?" campaign as a way to promote the studio's movies. That's like Martha Stewart paying K-Mart to pitch sheets.

With the clandestine work of only three associates, TNT organized the first annual Drammys. This internal awards program bestowed prizes on associates for the "Most Dramatic Moment," "Most Dramatic Celebrity Encounter," and "Most Dramatic E-mail." The award for the "Most Dramatic Meeting" went to the pregnant vice president of branding, whose water broke during a staff meeting. Jennifer Dorian, now called the "Drama Mama," gave birth to daughter Claudia the next day. A star is born. The Drammys were a hit and will now be held every year.

If communicating in emotion can be measured by associates keeled over in laughter and literally peeing in their pants, then Koonin accomplished his objective.

TNT's Drammys culminated in the crowning of a "Drama King" and "Drama Queen." And who was the inaugural Drama King at TNT?

Scot Safon.

Safon says that as he looks back at all the work that went into the brand initiative, he can see The Leader's Voice. "Everything was backed by the facts. Steve put an emotional overlay on it. Symbols were deployed."

Ask Steve Koonin how important communicating in facts, emotions, and symbols was to the success of TNT's brand initiative, and he'll give you a one-word response in his usual dramatic fashion.

"HUGE!"

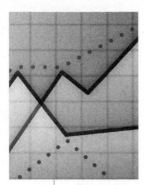

People
Love Facts

Chapter Four

Facts alone
seldom persuade
and **rarely inspire**

People love facts. We gobble and regurgitate sports statistics, weather data, calorie counts, business indicators, and gas prices. Factoid junkies play trivia parlor games. Audiences match abilities with contestants as they watch *Who Wants to Be a Millionaire*, *Win Ben Stein's Money*, or the aging king of trivia TV, *Jeopardy*. Investors breathlessly track the rise and fall of the Dow, Nasdaq, and S&P 500. We are media-bludgeoned by the latest facts on crime, trade imbalances, pollen counts, death tolls, hair loss, and box office records. Some people will never know who won last night's game, while others know individual player's middle names, scoring average, lifetime league ranking, and high school mascot. A man might say, "She's in her sixth month or so" when referring to a pregnancy. A woman would say, "She's in day two of her twenty-fourth week." Even though individuals track different facts or track facts differently, the reality is we are all tuned to the factual channel.

The Internet is a 24/7 buffet of facts. Spies and children alike can use the CIA's splendid World Factbook online as an A to Z resource. Anyone heading to Austria can learn that it is 83,858 square kilometers in size and located 47°20' north latitude and 13°20' east longitude. The CIA adds depth and understanding through comparison and description. Austria, a "landlocked republic," "slightly smaller than Maine" is in "Central Europe, north of Italy." Zambia is "slightly larger than Texas."

"PG at 84.99, MSFT at 60.23, and WWF at 13.40." Like corporate acronyms, these data remain meaningless until the lingo is learned and the context known. WWF at 13.40 alone means little. Knowing that the stock was up thirteen cents on February 15, 2002, because of Hulk Hogan's return to *WrestleMania* increases the meaning. Running back Corey Dillon carried the ball 315 times for 1,435 yards for a very respectable average of 4.6 yards per carry during the 2001 NFL season. Those are the facts. Unfortunately the 4 and 12 Cincinnati Bengals were the context. Facts are meaningless without context or interpretation.

Worshiping at the Altar of Data

Total Quality Management, TQM, changed business. It proved that databased decision making improves the quality of products and processes, while often reducing the cost of both. It taught a generation of business workers the importance of measuring things well and the usefulness of stockpiling data. Companies like NCR's Teradata provide monster databases to help business leaders warehouse facts.

The world is full of databases big and small. The U.S. government is using databases to identify criminals and track down terrorists. Companies like Wal-Mart invest millions of dollars in databases that track every purchase. On Amazon.com, buy a copy of the *Guinness Book of Records* and the online retailer's database will instantly tell you "customers who bought this book also bought" *The World Almanac and Book of Facts* and *Bias: A CBS Insider Exposes How the Media Distort the News,* by Bernard Goldberg.

Data mining now extracts previously unorganized but useful information from the stockpiles. Energy companies use Knowledge Discovery and Data Mining (KDD) to find oil in wells considered dry, and casinos now send free airline tickets to compulsive gamblers.

Einstein said, "Perfection of means and confusion of ends seem to characterize our age." In our new data-rich world, we find ourselves working like Bob Cratchit recording inputs and Ebenezer Scrooge counting outputs—all the while missing the meaning of our data and our work. Data warehousing and data mining are essential business means, but these means do not define the ends.

"Facts are the air of science," said Russian psychologist and Nobel Laureate Ivan Pavlov. "Without them you can never fly. Do not become archivists of facts, try to penetrate to the secret of their occurrence, persistently search for the laws that govern them."

Factual types of information include data, measures, numbers, trends, evidence, opinions, reasoned judgments, and numerical analysis. Facts teach, persuade, and entertain. Facts can be distorted, misrepresented, and illogically used to support dubious conclusions. Business leaders often communicate only facts and presume that others will share their interpretation. PLEASE presume they will not.

Some Facts Obscure the Truth

Worldwide research firm IDC carefully calculates that 38 million Americans are online; MediaQuest insists the number is 53 million; and IntelliQuest proclaims there are 73 million online. The CIA World Factbook reveals 148 million users. Evaluating a market opportunity using conflicting facts such as these is why market research is often regarded as oxymoronic.

Some Facts Are Difficult to Believe

"The average American is targeted by 3,000 messages per day. That includes phone calls, e-mail, meetings, conversations," writes David Shenk in *Data Smog: Surviving the Information Glut*. First, we wondered how Shenk derived the data. It sounded difficult to estimate what constitutes an "average American." Next, we pondered how we would confirm this through research. And last, we wanted to know how he defined a "message." Because of all this, we found Shenk's data difficult to believe.

Some Facts Are False

Take the case of the 56K modem. First, the FCC mandates a maximum 53K dial-up speed. Second, 53K is theoretical. Most of the time 46K is all that a person gets. Third, 56K is the number for *receiving* only. A 56K modem *sends* at 33K. Similar concepts apply to the one-, five-, and ten-year published rates on mutual funds. Maybe this is why our 401(k) is now a 201(k).

Some Facts Get Twisted

Author and Ph.D. Joel Best showcases a factual "transformation" in his book *Damned Lies and Statistics: Untangling Numbers from the Media, Politicians, and Activists.* "Every year since 1950, the number of American children gunned down has doubled." A Ph.D. candidate used this statistic to open his dissertation, and his advisory committee accepted the thesis without challenge. The student innocently quoted this "fact" verbatim from another source that Best chooses not to cite.

As Best did, let's crunch some numbers. If ten children had been shot in 1950, then in 1970, 10,485,760 children would have been slain. By 1973, the number would have jumped to 83,886,080. By 1995, 350 trillion (rounding to the nearest 10 trillion) children would be shot each year.

The original statistic, reported by the Children's Defense Fund in 1994, is "The number of American children killed each year by guns has doubled *since* 1950." This fact, transformed accidentally, we presume, then quoted innocently leads to incredulity.

Some Facts Get White-Washed

Business leaders are often guilty of factual euphemism. A 1995 op-ed piece in the *Wall Street Journal* tried to help people "crack the CEO code":

> "We had positive results" actually means "Our losses were less than last year."

> "We had an excellent year before special charges" actually means "we had to write down some dumb moves."

> "The year was a challenge" actually means "competitors are eating our lunch."

> "Through restructuring we're getting back to basics" actually means "no more ill-advised acquisitions, we're going to sell what we make best."

Some Facts Can Be Interpreted Differently

Michael Wood is vice president of Teen Research Unlimited (TRU). In his job, Michael is responsible for the twice-annual TRU Study that interviews 2,000 teens across the United States. More than 150 of the country's top brands and companies subscribe to the study, such as Target, Procter & Gamble, Cartoon Network, Kellogg, Polaroid, Sony Music, Sega, and the NFL. Two years ago, Michael said they asked teens what they would do with $100. The number one answer that came back was that teens would save the money. "Our first response was that this is great," he said. "Teens are fiscally responsible and are planning for the future. That's a good thing."

However, with further research in focus groups, the truth became evident. "They were saving the money because they wanted to spend it on something that cost more than $100." The teens weren't interested in fiscal responsibility; they wanted clothing, a new stereo, computer, and other more expensive stuff.

Facts can have multiple interpretations. "Left with just the raw data, we didn't know whether they were saving it and being prudent or just saving up to buy something more."

Some Facts Can Be Ignored

During an interview on *Meet the Press,* NBC's Tim Russert referred to a graph while asking Secretary of the Treasury Paul O'Neill about taxes. O'Neill responded, "I think people can endlessly make charts and, you know, add numbers and subtract numbers and whatever other magic you want to do." While O'Neill's statement is true, Russert's question was ignored and his 3.6 million viewers did not get an answer. Secretary O'Neill didn't just gloss over the facts, he slid right by them.

Communicating Facts

Leaders rely on facts to make decisions; they want their constituents to understand the facts so that they will more effectively contribute their intelligence to the decision-making process. Part of this process is exploring and organizing all the available facts. The critical moment comes when facts must be communicated either from the bottom up or the top down.

Communicating facts well requires the same skill as good storytelling.

Unfortunately, it's often the communication that fails rather than the facts. Yes, facts can obscure the truth, become twisted, and lead to multiple interpretations, but the communication is often the perpetrator.

There is in the business world an entire industry devoted to understanding facts and communicating them. Feasibility consultants look at all the facts and the kitchen sink. Whether it's looking at a new mixed-use development or a new restaurant, they study population, average household size, income, families, median age, racial characteristics, competing businesses, and all the financial numbers, such as per capita costs. And the list goes on and on.

As you can imagine, making sense of all these facts and communicating them clearly and concisely is quite a challenge. The founding father of the feasibility industry is Harrison "Buzz" Price. The eightysomething Buzz still prepares up to ten reports a year. For the last twenty-two years he has run the Harrison Price Company. Before that, he founded Economics Research Associates. He got his start at Stanford Research Institute in the 1950s. It was there that one of his professors first taught him about communicating facts. "He taught us how to create great graphics that could jump out of your head."

The secret, according to Buzz, is to use numbers to tell a great story. "The x and y axis are great tuners of communication."

For a numbers guy, it was interesting to listen to Buzz talk about communication. When he talks about numbers, metaphors roll off his tongue. He describes them as musical notes, a living language, points on an economic map, and signals. To him, understanding numbers is like economic geography. Communicating the facts is like taking people on a journey.

Buzz communicates with great emotion about numbers. "They make me wake up in the middle of the night and say 'OH!' Even when I don't have to pee." Actually, Buzz says *emotion* is the wrong word. "You have to be passionate about your numbers. You have to be in the right spirit of it."

We talked to some of his colleagues, and this is what they had to say about his communication skills:

"He's got the Technicolor to go with the numbers."

"He shoots arrows as straight as they can go."

"A tremendous number of other feasibility people love to obfuscate what they do. Buzz goes right to the heart of it."

"He's an outstanding communicator. Very precise and concise."

Buzz is a legend for a variety of reasons. He's conducted or managed more than six thousand feasibility studies. He's been roasted, toasted, and inducted more times than he'd like to remember. The sheer fact that in his eighties he still works is impressive enough. However, Buzz is probably most famous for his first client.

In 1955, he got a phone call from a "movie guy." A few weeks later, he was standing in an Anaheim orange grove. Buzz was paid $25,000 and given eight weeks to find the location for Disneyland. From the start, he said three potential locations were identified—the San Fernando Valley, the Pomona-San Gabriel area, and somewhere along the planned I-5 corridor. Buzz evaluated a host of dimensions. Among other things, he took temperatures and analyzed smog levels and growth patterns. At the end of the evaluation process, he prepared a report for Walt Disney.

As we peppered Buzz to tell us about communicating with Walt Disney, he spoke in the same language he always does. In other words, the same principles that work for a small developer in the Midwest work for Walt. "I cut through the chaos of numbers and cut right to the chase." In this case, it was to communicate that Anaheim was the best place for Walt to build Disneyland.

Buzz worked for years with Walt, but he never joined the Walt Disney Company. Both knew it was best for the "strategic planner" to be outside. It insulated Buzz from the management structure at Disney. As he told Walt then, "You won't listen to me if I'm on the payroll."

While Walt Disney's great successes are well chronicled, some of his ideas were shelved because the numbers didn't support them. Some of the 110 studies he conducted were, in his own words, "negative." There was the attraction at Niagara Falls and an indoor park in St. Louis. Buzz also looked at locations near Washington, D.C., and Palm Beach, Florida, for the company's second major theme park, Disney World.

There is a naïve business fallacy that suggests statistics establish facts. However, we believe that leaders understand that the reverse is true. Leaders assert a goal, vision, and/or agenda and then test for statistical likelihood. They allow facts to inform their interpretation so they can improve decision making and communication.

Some More Tips

Communicating facts well is far more difficult than regurgitating data. It requires the same skill as good storytelling. The following ideas will help you turn the factual channel into more than just a connection to a database.

Facts Are Not Boring, But You Might Be

Numbers are the language of business. Unfortunately it is a boring language

Numbers are the language of business. Unfortunately it is a boring language when spoken by most leaders.

when spoken by most leaders. Reading data aloud to groups, especially in monotone, is B-O-O-O-R-I-N-G. Displaying stacks of facts during a presentation or in writing can bore. Constituents soon tune out because they can read faster than you can speak or write your thoughts. Worse, they may conclude that you have not analyzed the data.

The leader's communication job is more *interpretation* than *recitation*. Minimal data presentation and maximum interpretation usually converts boring to interesting. Stand ready to share the larger collection of facts that influenced your decision, but showcase your thinking, not the data for data's sake. This applies to written communication, too.

Make Facts Memorable

A simple analogy can make data understandable and memorable. For example, an acre is about the size of a football field, and a gigabyte of information is about the size of one thousand average-length novels. Professor Chip Heath, a Stanford-trained psychologist says:

> People do care about the truth of an idea, but they also want to tell stories that produce strong emotion, and that second tendency sometimes gets in the way of the first. If we could understand what kinds of stories succeed beyond all expectations, even when they are not true, we might be able to take legitimate information, about health for example, and change people's behavior for the better.
>
> Or if I were a business manager, I would love to have a mission statement for my organization that was as successful at moving through the organization as the most successful urban legends. Much evidence suggests that people are very poor at remembering facts such as statistics, while they are better at remembering and repeating ideas cast as narratives or as analogies. This is hard for our MBA students to accept, because I think business people in general think that facts speak for themselves.

Bill Gates appeared to be a poor representative for Microsoft when he was called before the Justice Department. However, he hit a home run when he said that demanding that Microsoft remove its browser from Windows is like telling automotive companies to remove radios from their cars because it might put radio manufacturers out of business.

Metaphors and color help make communication memorable. "The companies that succeed will be the ones that make their ideas real, that stand for what is true, and that employ great metaphors and analogies to define their businesses and tell their stories," said Sun Microsystems CEO Scott McNealy. "After all, cash and coin notwithstanding, money itself is merely an agreed-upon representation of that other great truth: value. And I can assure you, value is real."

Even fact addicts resort to metaphor. One recent article about KDD suggested, "Metadata maintenance is as essential as car maintenance—if you forget to fill up your car and don't inflate your tires, very soon your car will run out of gas or will have an accident."

Stanford students Heath and Jonah Berger scanned publication databases to track the proliferation of the two most repeated phrases from the 2000 presidential debates. They were Gore's "Lockbox" and Bush's "Fuzzy Math" metaphors. Fuzzy Math won by a narrow margin.

Use pictures or word pictures. In 1921 the national advertising manager for Street Railways Advertising Company, Fredrick R. Barnard, composed the phrase, "One look is worth a thousand words." He later modified this to "ten thousand words." The adage *A picture is worth a thousand words* is the common adaptation of his original phrase. According to courtroom guru and Cincinnati attorney Lou Gilligan, "The right picture is worth $100,000 in the courtroom." Any way you slice it, a picture has value.

Make Facts Stick through Humor

The U.S. standard railroad gauge is four feet, eight and one-half inches. How did we wind up with such an odd railway width? Because that was the width English railroad-building expatriates brought with them to America. Why did the English build them this wide? Because the first British rail lines were built by the same people who built the pre-railroad tramways, and that's the gauge they used. Why did they use that gauge?

Because the same jigs, tools, and people who built wagons built the tramways and used the standard wagon-wheel spacing. Wagon-wheel spacing was standardized due to a very practical, hard-to-change and easy-to-match reality. When Britain was ruled by Imperial Rome, Roman war chariots, in true bureaucratic fashion, all used a standard spacing between their wheels. Over time, this spacing left deep ruts along the extensive road network the Romans built. If British wheel spacing didn't match Roman ruts, the wheels would break.

The Roman standard was derived after trial-and-error efforts of early wagon and chariot builders. They determined the best width that would accommodate two horse butts was four feet, eight and one-half inches. Thus the United States standard railroad gauge is a hand-me-down standard based upon the original specification for an Imperial Roman war chariot.

This doesn't end at railroads. Two big booster rockets attach to the sides of the main fuel tank that lifts the Space Shuttle into orbit. Thiokol makes these solid-fuel rocket boosters, SRBs, at its Utah factory. The engineers who design the SRBs ship them from factory to launch site by train. The railroad line from the factory runs through a mountain tunnel only slightly wider than the railroad track. Even if Thiokol engineers wanted fatter SRBs, the railway gauge limits their design. Modern space chariot design follows horses' butts. Specifications and bureaucracies live forever, leading one to wonder about ISO standards.

Display Facts

We agree with Edward Tufte, who asserts that graphics are not "devices for showing the obvious to the ignorant." While a variety of software has granted permission to the graphical Michelangelo that lives in every businessperson, distorting data unintentionally because this impish internal artist insists on color, depth, and impact only makes you appear to be an amateur. It is nearly impossible to communicate business ideas and issues without supporting charts, tables, or graphs. Visually expressing the meaning (perhaps the poetry) of numbers is a daunting task, whether written or during oral presentation. Learn to display data well.

When using The Leader's Voice, our advice concerning graphical display is simple. Graphical displays either share data or aid you as you persuade others to accept your point of view. The facts should be accurate, clear, and support the interpretation. The title of the chart should state the point you are making. The chart itself should be simple enough to be understood by the average high school student. Leave the glitz to Las Vegas.

A great example that demonstrates these principles is *The First Measured Century: An Illustrated Guide to Trends in America, 1900-2000,* by Theodore Caplow, Louis Hicks, and Ben J. Wattenberg, published by the American Enterprise Institute Press.

Turn Facts into a Story

Fact: Iron ore mines in northern Minnesota reduced in number from 284 to 7, while the employees reduced 48,000 to 6,700 from 1960 to 2000.

Or, you could say it this way . . .

> "Most of the iron ore in the United States comes from the Mesabi mountain range north of Duluth. Glaciers ground an old ridge to form these gentle rolling mounds of free iron ore. In 1960, we had 284 mines and approximately 48,000 mine employees up there, pounding the mountain into rubble. By 2000, there were only 7 mines and 6,700 employees. Yet, we mined about 50 million tons of ore every year for forty years. We started with lots of people and small machines, and now we do it with fewer people and monster machines."

These are the words of Thomas Peluso, vice president and general manager of National Steel Pellet Company in Keewatin, Minnesota. Peluso spoke softly as he told us about the dramatic changes he had witnessed firsthand. He had worked his way up from an overall-wearing miner to a tie-wearing executive.

We could continue talking about the lives and communities that were impacted, but hopefully you get the picture. A little context can add a lot of meaning.

Add Sparkle with Amazing Facts

Using amazing facts can alter viewpoints in an instant. Amazing facts are the diamonds found in mountains of data. They can at once convey facts, emotion, and symbols as they cause a person's mind to rapidly fill in the blanks. Try some of these on for size.

Eighty-seven percent of all sales leads are never pursued.

More than 90 percent of all HIV infections are in sub-Sahara Africa. If the cure were a single glass of clean water, most would not have access to it.

The Centers for Disease Control reports that more than 90,000 people per year die from hospital ERRORS. That's equivalent to a fully loaded 737 crashing every day—no survivors.

According to the U.S. Census Bureau, as of 1994:

> Black women with high school diplomas earn 3 percent more income than white women with high school diplomas.

> Black women with some college education earn 6 percent more income than white women with some college education.

> Black women who are college graduates earn 7 percent more income than white women who are college graduates.

Summary

Facts provide the underpinning logic to a message. Most leaders understand the facts but do not often take the time to create a compelling, memorable representation of what the facts mean. Like a TV business correspondent, they report the data in a commanding series of sound bites and then believe their constituency understands the world as they do. Even an emotional appeal cannot rescue facts delivered without context or interpretation. Disengagement and recurring bouts of cynicism cause constituents to reject flimsy sound bites that babble past tough issues. Constituents will interpret the facts and combine them with their own emotions and symbols to create meaning. A leader who knows how to use facts is powerful. Good factual communication builds trust and fosters confidence.

These are the facts, as we see them.

Tune in to Emotions

Chapter Five

We follow
leaders because
of how they make us
feel.

Near both our homes in the Cincinnati suburbs stands one of the icons of the golden age of broadcasting. Built by radio and television tycoon Powel Crosley Jr., the diamond-shaped WLW radio tower stands a whopping 831 feet above the surrounding newly developed neighborhoods. On May 2, 1934, FDR turned a gold key in the White House, unleashing the tower's 500,000 watts. It was a signal so strong that WLW became known as "The Nation's Station."

A large pond was constructed next to the tower to supply the 1,200 gallons of water per minute needed to cool the twenty 100,000-watt tubes. Nearby residents literally could listen to WLW on their toasters, faucets, and dental work. Even today, at the FCC's maximum allowed 50,000 watts, the powerful station can be heard from Detroit to Birmingham.

Emotions are the wattage of leadership communication. To broadcast with full power and a clear channel, you must know and reveal your true emotions. As a leader, you must also know and articulate constituents' important but unspoken feelings. Finally, you must foster passionate alignment around shared aspirations.

Constituents constantly scan the emotional channel, tuning in to stations that inspire, encourage, and engage. They listen to talk shows that articulate what they believe, popular music that stirs their soul, and up-to-the-minute news and weather. They have preprogrammed buttons that help them find favorite stations and bypass others they hate. Question is "Are they tuning you *in* or *out?*"

The best leaders broadcast on several of the following stations. The first stop on our emotional radio dial is WFEL—Feelings, featuring basic human emotions.

WFEL — Feelings

Carrie O'Neal, our talented art director, recently brought her four-month-old baby, Abby, to the office. We all stopped working. We gathered around this gorgeous, clearly above-average child like jewelers around the Hope Diamond. We wanted to hold Abby. We made weird faces, spoke goo-goo, da-da, and beamed. Babies bring out emotions in all of us.

Psychologists agree there is a basic set of emotions, even though they do not agree upon the exact set. Love, hope, sadness, anger, happiness, just like primary colors, are all part of the leader's palette. By communicating these basic emotions, leaders remind constituents that they are viewed as human beings, not business components. Professors Christopher Bartlett and Sumantra Ghoshal, writing in the *Sloan Management Review,* suggest that leaders should refrain from assuming "loyalty is dead" and rise to the challenge of attracting and energizing their constituents. Management expert Peter Drucker, in *Harvard Business Review,* says, "Leaders need to emotionally connect to the often overlooked, growing number of temporary workers they employ."

During her tenure as head of the Body Shop, Anita Roddick pushed to make her company "braver, cleverer, gutsier." Like ice cream entrepreneurs "Ben & Jerry," she deliberately tied business ideas to the everyday social and environmental issues many people feel deeply about. Martin Luther King Jr. connected on a personal level when he expressed his dream that "my four little children will one day live in a nation where they will not be judged by the color of their skin but by the content of their character." Hillary Rodham Clinton emotionally connects with her constituents by talking about the world as a village with everyone helping to raise its children. When President George W. Bush climbed into the stands to sit with the athletes at the Opening Ceremonies of the 2002 Olympic Winter Games in Salt Lake City, it was clear that he was just as excited to sit with them as they were to sit with him. Former New York Governor Mario Cuomo shared his heart during the riveting keynote address to the 1984 Democratic National Convention. He appealed to everyday hopes and dreams by telling us how his parents taught him the American dream: "I learned about our kind of democracy from my father. And I learned about our obligation to each other from him and my mother. They asked only for a chance to work and to make the world better for their children."

Amazon.com's Jeff Bezos's 2000 letter to the shareholders begins simply with, "Ouch. It's been a brutal year." The CEO's ability to connect on an everyday level with people is part of his genius. This simple expression allowed him to list the facts of the previous year's struggles with greater effect. To help shareholders place their financial fears in perspective, he later quotes investor Benjamin Graham, "In the short term, the stock market is a voting machine; in the long term, it's a weighing machine."

KPOW — The Power Station

Leaders appeal to our best selves and our most noble desires. In *Reflections of a Public Man,* former Texas Representative Jim Wright writes about the early days of the civil rights movement. It was 1957, only three years after *Brown vs. Board of Education,* and waves of anger, fear, and resentment still surged throughout much of the South. He remembers struggling over his vote on one of the first civil rights bills in Congress since the Reconstruction.

Speaker of the House and fellow Texan Sam Rayburn appealed to him with these words: "Jim, I think you want to vote for this bill. I'm sure you have been receiving a lot of angry, bitter mail against it. I believe you are strong enough to withstand and overcome any such opposition as that. And I know that in the future you will be proud that you did."

"He was right on all four points," observed Wright. "A full generation later, I honor his memory for having believed the best about me and appealing to me in a way that showed he did."

Jim Kouzes and Barry Posner, authors of the best-selling *The Leadership Challenge,* understand that leadership is a relationship. Working with them over the past fifteen years, we and our colleagues have asked more than one hundred thousand individuals to describe how leaders' words and actions contribute to constituents' feelings of power.

This personal experience of a mid-level IT manager is typical of the stories we have heard. "My boss invited me into her office and said, 'The Lincoln project is our top priority and could become a significant economic engine for us. We need our best talent, someone with guts, intellect, and perseverance to head it up. This project was originally my idea and is very important to me.

THE EMOTIONAL CHANNEL

I believe in it. I'll support this idea, win or lose, but I plan on winning. I only have one question for you. Will you lead it?' I felt terrific that she would have such faith in me. I took the leap and said *yes*." The IT manager now talks about it as one of the best leadership experiences of her life.

The word "empowerment" bugs us and we don't believe in it. You can grant authority, assign responsibility, and support decisions, but power is not something you give to someone else. We empower ourselves because we already have the power within us. Leaders can help constituents find their own power. A leader's words of belief and support can fan confident embers into powerful flames. Faking these kinds of statements leads to disaster. So you have to ask yourself, "Do I really believe in people?" Ultimately, leadership is an act of faith in other people.

KOUR — Encouragement

We are willing to bet that you have kept a letter, note or token of congratulation, praise or thanks for a job well done. We have found that roughly 85 percent of business people have such a "thank you" and many have kept them for years. We have a few, and like you, we know exactly where they are even though we have not looked at them for a while. Why? Because of how they made us feel.

We all want to believe that we count, that we matter, that our work matters, and that our contribution helps to make things better. Recognition and expressions of appreciation, whether hand-written notes or public praise, confirm our hope that our work counts.

We are passionate capitalists. That said, money has little to do with recognition. Of the thousands of stories we have heard about individuals' most meaningful recognition, few have anything to do with money. Even when big money and big trips were involved, the money was not what they remembered most. It's like Jennifer Dorian's Drammy award for the "Most Dramatic Moment" at TNT. The cheap plastic Oscaresque statuette is displayed prominently in the one place where everyone can see it as they pass by her office.

KHOP — Hope and Optimism

Any sales manager knows that optimism is a key indicator for sales success. In his book *Learned Optimism*, Martin Seligman shares an experience he had with John Creedon, CEO of Metropolitan Life Insurance Company.

Creedon had been concerned about the human toll in his business. Fifty percent of his salespeople washed out within a year or so. He wanted to know if there was a better way to select candidates. Seligman's book outlines what all leaders need to know about promoting optimism. Pessimistic people will say permanent, pervasive, and personal things to themselves like, "I've never been any good at this," "No one likes me," or "I can't get my boss to notice me." This type of self-talk leads to early defeat and then perhaps to permanent defeat. We know leaders who say the same kinds of things to their constituents.

Leaders who explain things in temporary, specific, and external ways promote greater optimism: "The market is down, but it always comes back." "They already have a brand agency, but they need a good one like ours." "We didn't make our numbers, but no one did after 9/11."

The same principles apply to leaders. Don't browbeat your staff or remind them that they are always behind. Avoid giving them the impression that the situation will never change or that they are dolts. Instead, communicate in less permanent, less pervasive, and less personal ways to promote healthy optimism. As Seligman writes, "Finding temporary and specific causes for misfortune is the art of hope. Finding permanent and universal causes for misfortunes is the practice of despair."

KNGY — Pure Energy

Our business partner, Tom Peters, is consistently one of the world's highest-paid business speakers. Tom's speeches are passionate rants about the glories and failures of business. His three-*S* oratorical style—sweating, swearing, and spitting—keeps those of us who know him best off the front row. *BusinessWeek* describes him as business' "best friend and worst nightmare." Social commentator Dinesh D'Souza, in *The Virtue of Prosperity,* calls Tom, "One of the founding members of the Party of Yea, a cheerleader-in-chief for the New Economy." People not only appreciate Tom's genius, they also love his passion about business. Tom's metaphors and stories nail what all of us are thinking and feeling but are unable to articulate. His energy and passion are key factors in his consistent rating as the most credible business voice alive.

We love Tom's style, but it's Tom's style. The great French intellect François Marie Arouet de Voltaire said, "Any style that is not boring is a good one." Often energy has little to do with volume or charisma, just as READ-ING THIS IN ALL CAPS may mean nothing. A pep rally leadership formula cannot sustain success. Besides, the engineers, programmers, and accountants won't show up unless you have free beer.

We know many soft-spoken leaders whose energy is communicated through their untiring work ethic, observable commitment, continuous interaction with constituents, and their unrelenting pursuit of the organization's success. In a world where everyone is shouting, the quiet voice may be the most distinct.

We believe that constituents will readily forgive most leadership faults. However, a lack of energy is seldom forgiven because it is perceived as a lack of caring or commitment. It's like the manager we once knew who was so emotionally flat that his team referred to him as, "The suit with nobody in it." They couldn't find his station anywhere on the dial.

KEMP — Empathy

Psychologist and educator Howard Gardner described empathy as "the ability to notice and make distinctions among other individuals and, in particular, among their moods, temperaments, motivations and intentions." Empathy is about understanding the emotions of an individual or a group.

For example, Herb Kelleher empathized with an entire industry and nation in the Southwest Airlines 2001 annual report to shareholders. "For the airline industry this was not merely Dante's purgatory. It was, indeed, Dante's pure 'hell,' created in one amazing and tragic day."

Listening through the factual, emotional, and symbolic channels is a powerful way to understand others and connect at deeper levels. So, when listening to others, ask for the facts. Listen for emotions and then confirm how others feel and why they feel that way. Finally, pay close attention to the symbols that people use.

Leaders are often unaware of the negative impact they have both on the group and on individual constituents. Our research with Kouzes and Posner describes how leaders sometimes treat individuals. "Not being listened to," "having no influence," and "having no voice in the matter," are common statements we have repeatedly heard. This lack of empathy in action silenced constituents, reducing their effectiveness.

In a world where everyone is shouting, the quiet voice may be the most distinct.

 — Emoting

Describing his transformation at LensCrafters, Dave Browne said, "I really felt like I was living two lives. At home and church I had love and respect in my life. At work it was only about numbers and winning. The day I realized I could bring these emotions from my personal life to work, my business relationships improved and so did our results."

When talking about leadership, Dave can't go two sentences without using the words "head" and "heart" together. He describes his change as the beginning of a "real romance." After years of dividing his emotions, he really changed. Speaking of LensCrafters' three-day, ten-year anniversary celebration, he said, "I cried, I laughed, I hugged and I danced. I put my tears and fears right out there." The results of adding an emotional channel to his great factual channel led to Dave and his team building LensCrafters into the most successful niche retailer in the United States.

Communication expert Kathleen Hall Jamieson writes, "Scholars of interpersonal communication tell us that openness invites openness; disclosure, disclosure. Self-disclosure can accelerate our sense of intimacy in a relationship." Growing up, children learn to protect themselves from emotional injury, feeling embarrassed, inadequate, or sounding stupid. To some, emotional distance equals safety. At the extreme, this cuts people off from their own emotions. If the adage "don't let them see you sweat" is your heroic way of saying "don't let them see anything," then you have likely gone too far. Unable to understand your own emotions, you become incapable of appropriately revealing them to others.

The key word here is "appropriately." It is naïve to believe that we should share all of our emotions all of the time. We once heard, "Don't tell people your problems. Eighty percent don't care and the other 20 percent are glad you've got them." Of course, leaders can hide some emotions and remain authentic. The question is which emotions should you share and which do you keep to yourself? Hide most of your anger, depression, cynicism, and disappointment. Notice we say "most." Letting people know when you are frustrated, disappointed, or dispirited can strengthen relationships. However, chronic complaining and blaming disqualifies you as a leader. Everyone wants to believe in something, so share your optimism, hope, and passion. People tune in to uplifting stations.

KMDY — Comedy

Humor can be used to increase social ties; gain approval; manage stress, fear, and embarrassment; invite participation into tough issues; and even attack the opposition. When it is part of a leader's natural repertoire, humor can even reframe dire moments. The nation relaxed a little when after President Ronald Reagan was shot, he quipped to his wife, Nancy, "Honey, I forgot to duck," and to the doctors, "Please tell me you're Republicans."

However, using humor only to call attention to oneself nearly always causes constituents to turn the dial. In leadership communication, poking fun at others can also be dangerous territory. Beware of humor that chafes rather than charms. Here are a couple simple yet effective examples of leaders using humor:

> Speaking at the European Policy Centre on January 28, 2002, General Electric Company Chairman and CEO Jeff Immelt spoke about his new job and GE's failed merger with Honeywell. "This is my first visit to Brussels since becoming Chairman of GE. You told my predecessor, Jack Welch, to 'go home' last June; by the way, I told him to 'go home' in September!"

During a slew of speeches on the proposed HP/Compaq merger, Hewlett-Packard CEO Carly Fiorina spoke at the Goldman Sachs Technology Conference on Monday, February 4, 2002. "It's great to be here this morning. I haven't had the opportunity to address a room full of institutional investors since, well, Friday. I was having withdrawals."

The difference between a comedian and a humorist is the difference between a joke and a funny story. David Greatbatch and Timothy Clark, of King's College, University of London, studied the use of humor and public speaking. They observed that internationally acclaimed business speakers create humor during their presentations through jokes, quips, and stories, with a majority of their humor conveyed through stories.

The difference between a speaker and a leader is the difference between entertainment and alignment. The most effective humor has purpose.

WACT — Actions

Actions speak louder than words. Tom Smith is the CEO of VHA, a 2,200-member national network of community-owned health care systems and their physicians. A complex, distributed network with highly independent regional units all working in one of the world's most confusing and frustrating industries on the planet, it is simply the most complicated business we have ever worked with. While Tom has a compelling vision, he is followed because he is a compelling leader. Tom is not a pulpit-pounding televangelist. A dignified, quiet-spoken man, his words are straightforward and powerful. Tom's emotional channel communication comes primarily through his actions. He is so trusted that his communication bypasses the usual filters—the filters that cause us to ask if he means what he says, will he follow through, and does he care about the organization and me. His words and actions combine to create a powerful emotional station.

The three most exciting roller coasters in the world are . . . No. 3, the Magnum XL-200 at Cedar Point in Sandusky, Ohio. At No. 2 . . . the Thunderbolt at Kennywood Park near Pittsburgh. And, the No. 1 most exciting roller coaster in the world is . . . the semiconductor industry. While we are in a rating mood, on our "Favorite Leaders" list is Steve Hansen, CEO of ON Semiconductor in Phoenix, Arizona. ON is a Motorola spin-off that went

IPO just prior to the dot.com bubble bursting. After a spectacular career riding Motorola in the United States and Europe, he continued his thrills by plummeting along on Nasdaq with the rest of the high-tech world. The day after ON's first major layoff, Steve was in the cafeteria with other executives answering the tough questions with candor and sincerity. Working around the clock, he met with employees from all over the world, often by teleconference. The emotional tone of these meetings was genuine and absent the emotional manipulation lesser leaders use to get people back to work. Steve is "the real thing." The loyalty that follows Steve is due to his business excellence and the truthful way he shares his emotions.

Signing Off

We follow leaders because of how they make us feel. Yet the very process of becoming a leader creates emotional distance. Don Clarke encountered this dilemma at age thirty-eight. He was one of the youngest people ever to be promoted to chairman of a major division at the multibillion-dollar retailer, May Company. The day before taking the job full-time, his predecessor congratulated him and said, "Tomorrow two things will be true that are not true today. First, you will be the chairman. Second, you have heard the truth for the last time."

Before joining the Bush administration as Secretary of State, Colin Powell told executives that even in creating an "informal, open (and) collaborative" communication environment they will become isolated. "Prepare to be lonely," he counseled.

Constituents rarely provide negative feedback to executives about their communication. Even when leaders give a bad speech the public feedback is positive, sometimes glowing. A HayGroup survey found that, in general, "people are less inclined to give constructive feedback to higher-status individuals." A lack of truthful feedback widens emotional distance and erodes trust, which creates even more communication barriers. This fear of telling the truth reinforces the leader's natural need to feel that the communication was powerful and clear.

At this moment, if you are a senior leader, you may be thinking that communication disconnects are not entirely your fault. The truth is that nervous leaders, relieved by the positive feedback, would rather accept the praise than seek the truth. Without absolving constituents, we suggest that fixing the problem is still primarily your responsibility.

Symbols: Rabbit's Foot and Rosary

Chapter Six

The ring on your finger, the blue ribbon you saved, and the flower pressed in a book all mean something. Scouts name their pack, high schools choose mascots, families inherit crests, companies design logos, and nations raise flags. The stories we tell, the art we display, and the music we love are symbols of identity. Over time, emblems represent culture and are passed along to subsequent generations. Many symbols are timeless.

A symbol is as powerful as the action or emotion it evokes. We attach more symbols to things that are more important. Win a volleyball tournament and a trophy symbolizes victory. Graduation tassels, gowns, and diplomas signify years of academic achievement. Wedding vows, veils, rings, garters, bouquets, toasts, broken glass, things borrowed, and things blue celebrate the promise of love and commitment. Authors and scholars Joseph F. McConkie and Donald Parry accurately classify symbols as the "most articulate of all languages." Symbols are as natural as smiles, shrugs, and winks. They fuse emotion and logic to purchase valuable space in constituents' minds. A symbol is a communication shortcut that does the heavy lifting for both sender and receiver. It conveys mutual understanding and individual meaning at the same time.

A leader without symbols is like Elvis without hips. In addition to hips, business leaders use symbolic language to communicate their most important messages about brand, vision, values, and strategy. Anthropologist Ian Tattersall writes, "Language is, indeed, the ultimate symbolic mental function, and it is virtually impossible to conceive of thought as we know it in its absence." Some of us struggle to understand the idea of symbolic communication even as we use it. While we were talking about symbols with a computer scientist

From a rabbit's foot to a rosary, symbols
are the shortcuts to the great truths
that guide our lives.

at a U.S. National Lab, the man shrugged his shoulders in frustration. "I'm lost in the forest here," he said. "I just don't get this symbols stuff."

Superheroes, Science, and Symbols

During our research, we talked with a great brand leader who used symbols to teach science to a challenging audience. Heather Shirley is a brand manager for the German conglomerate Bayer A.G. and responsible for Midol, an over-the-counter pain-relief medication for women experiencing the "physical symptoms of premenstrual syndrome." While Midol is the number one drug in its market, Heather wanted a bigger piece of the $172 billion teen market by creating loyal teenage customers. She also wanted to serve the public interest by establishing Midol as a "trusted source of information about what's happening to their bodies." Armed with initial research, Heather decided to reach them online. Heather also knew that teenage girls were not going to surf for this kind of information. Most of the Internet's medical information is clinical and boring to teenagers. For example, *WebMD* explains:

> Nearly all women experience bloating, breast tenderness, and slight, temporary weight gain. . . . Other PMS symptoms may include gastrointestinal distress, headaches, rashes, muscle and joint pains, fatigue, gingivitis, heart pounding, imbalance, hot flashes, oversensitivity to sounds and smells, agitation, and insomnia. . . . Emotional hypersensitivity is common with PMS, and women report a wide range of related symptoms, including depression, anxiety, anger, and agitation. They also report impaired concentration and some memory loss . . .

"Today's teens are incredibly savvy and incredibly saturated with stimuli," Shirley said. "Simply preaching the brand message in a straightforward way would only make teens tune out." Continuing to immerse herself in the subject through focus groups and other research methods, Heather and her team decided to communicate via an animated interactive cartoon, quiz, and game on the Midol Web site. Animators from Chicago's *itoons* Corporation were chosen to help. *Itoons'* president and CEO, Norm Dwyer, said, "We were dealing with girls just hitting puberty who probably don't fully understand what is happening to their bodies. We wanted girls to be able to sit at the computer, giggle, and learn a little bit about what was happening."

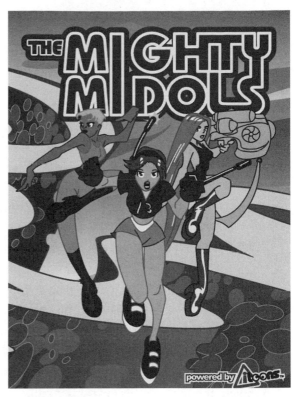

Midol's interactive game showed these teens how to overcome the "maddening minions of Monsteruation," namely bloating, aches, pains, and cramps. Teenage consumers are "sisters in trouble," battling these monsters. After *itoons* decided what "cramp monsters" looked like, superheroes were needed to defeat them. Shirley explains, "With the superhero symbols, we were able to deliver the empowering attitude we wanted young women to embrace." The Mighty Midols "came to life."

> Marissa Midol—Code Name: Cramp Killer
> Mimi Midol—Code Name: Water Retention Warrior
> Maya Midol—Code Name: PMS Predator

According to Heather Shirley, the superheroes are "young women who have strength, intelligence, great fashion sense, and they understand that being friends can get you through anything." In the game, the superheroes are manipulated by keyboard strokes that battle fatigue, bloats, and cramps. Blasting fatigue earns you 50 points; bloats bring in 100 points. Destroy the cramps and get 150 points! We played: Top score, 5,200.

"Power in friendship, strength in teamwork—the Mighty Midols embody the same skills young women are learning through school activities that will carry them far in life," Shirley said. "Plus, they're hanging out at the mall— what teen women can't relate to that?"

The campaign got teens listening and talking. The Mighty Midols have increased Web traffic by more than 20 percent, and page views by more than 30 percent.

> **If the leader does not define brand, vision, strategy, or agenda symbolically, constituents will.**

For most corporations, the brand is the most important symbol. Shapes, such as Coca-Cola's bottle, Nike's swoosh, or McDonald's golden arches, are brand emblems. Colors are important brand elements, like *National Geographic*'s yellow border and the brown trucks and uniforms of United Parcel Service. Rolls-Royce, Louis Vuitton, and M&Ms use stylized text to symbolize their brand. While business leaders will readily admit the importance of marketing symbolism, they often fail to deliberately use symbols to communicate other ideas. They'll spew the facts and even get emotional, but often forget to use symbols consciously and well. Their incomplete message forces followers to fill in the blanks.

Remember, the human brain uses facts, emotions, *and* symbols to create complete thoughts. Leaders may communicate well on one or two channels, but their audience naturally listens and thinks on all three channels. If the leader does not define brand, vision, strategy, or agenda symbolically, constituents will.

As you think about the following descriptions of symbols and how they are used, ask yourself whether your business symbols are allies or enemies. "Are they defined *by* you or *for* you?"

> Logos, word pictures, stories, anecdotes, myths, metaphors, legends, analogies, slogans, mottos, quotations, poems, creeds, examples, pictures, similes, parables, designs, equations, charts, graphs, colors, artifacts, lists, traditions, customs, shrines, insignias, celebrations, awards, perks, praises, ceremonies, rituals, heroes, music, theme songs, amazing facts, policies, statues, programs, certificates, organizational structures, flags, architectural blueprints, models, and humor.

From a rabbit's foot to a rosary, symbols are the shortcuts to the great truths that guide our lives. Finding symbols is a simple matter. Right now, wherever you are, stop, look around, and try to spot six symbols in twelve seconds. It might be easy for you to do this, but finding the best symbol and giving it life is a little tougher. We have some ideas that may aid you in developing meaningful symbols.

Prototype Symbols

Graphic designers and ad agencies create many initial ideas or symbolic prototypes when they are developing brand collateral such as logos, Web layouts, or annual reports. They quickly sketch and develop storyboards for many ideas at a conceptual level. Leaders can create symbolic communication prototypes the same way.

Inventors, artists, designers, and brand developers habitually immerse themselves in streams of stimuli. They use a variety of both standard and novel artifacts, pictures, games, or magazines to stimulate their own creativity. They play with ideas, make lists and draw pictures, and create divergent prototypes. Once they have enough, they stop using their creativity to *diverge* and start using it to *converge*. They narrow the field by comparing and contrasting the prototypes' merits. Ultimately they hone in on their best candidate. They select the final symbol by evaluating its impact, subtlety, feeling, color, scale, tone, durability, and other features.

Symbols by Immersion

Diving deeply into a single subject is another prototyping process. Rather than using an array of stimuli, narrow the field to a particular subject and become absorbed by it. Read everything you can find, live with it, sleep and eat with it. Do what Heather Shirley did. Talk to experts and novices on the subject. Because symbols are a natural part of life, they emerge naturally. Many people find that after a few days of immersion, they have a breakthrough moment and experience a flood of ideas and clarity.

Eclectic Research

Look for business metaphors in nonbusiness publications. *Scientific American* might lead you to compare your new knowledge management system to a supernova or a black hole. *National Geographic* might show how tribal chiefs use symbolism to maintain alignment. As soon as you finish this business book, read a nonbusiness book. Conduct online searches for interesting topics or people. We discovered some dizzying, innovative ideas for adult education and e-learning as we walked past seven miles of exhibits at the International Association of Amusement Parks and Attractions (IAAPA) annual convention in Orlando. Our evening at Universal Studios' "Islands of Adventure" offered a smorgasbord of symbols—from the eclectic theming of the entry plaza to the dazzling special effects of *The Amazing Adventures of Spider-Man*. More experiences equal more symbols in your communication. You can't say "life is like a box of chocolates" unless you've eaten a few boxes of them yourself.

Many of the best communicators we have observed or interviewed have a lifelong reading habit they support. Or they are constantly in conversation with interesting people from outside their immediate business interests. Reading one book or speaking with one person may not alter your perspective, but reading one hundred books or speaking with one hundred interesting people will.

Reference This

We have a stack of reference books and a long list of favorite Web sites containing information on synonyms, aphorisms, quotations, word origins, phrase origins, biographies, philosophical terms, and speech topics. For example, the phrase "hang out" was very popular in the 1830s. It referred to the custom of socializing in the neighborhood where your trade shingle was hung. The term "big cheese" is an interpretation of the Urdu word *chiz,* meaning "thing." As this phrase traveled from colonial India to Britain, it changed to mean "something good." Not quite what it means today.

Several years ago we were delivering some tough "360 feedback" to an executive team and needed a spoonful of sugar. Turning to our stack of books, we found a reference to feedback being a gift. We worked with the metaphor to include two kinds of wrapping paper—brightly colored for praise, and plain brown for criticism. We extended the idea by urging the executives to send thank-you notes to the giver. This simple metaphor helped create the right environment and eased the group's resistance so they could receive the "gift." It's now a staple for us.

With the Internet, we have the ultimate guide to references. Ask Google about feedback, and you can find a quotation from Brigadier General Ted Mercer Jr.: "Feedback is a gift. It's a way of giving help, and it's a corrective mechanism for people who want to learn how well their behavior matches their intentions." At **www.theleadersvoice.biz** we have links to our favorite sources.

Ask Marketing

Advertising agencies, brand development companies, and marketing pros are the symbolic communication gurus. Ask your marketing department for help. It is what they do. Recruit four creative crazies to play with your ideas, looking for the right symbolism. Take the political cartoonist from your local paper to lunch. Listen to your kids' vernacular and ask for definitions, dude.

You will miss sometimes. Even brand masters miss the mark once in a while. The Leo Burnett agency is one of the masters. Its founder, the late Leo Burnett, had a distinct way of thinking: "It seems to us there should be less concern about the dimensions of a business. And considerably more concern about its heartbeat—the values, zest, and spirit behind its physical and financial facade."

The Burnett agency created the U.S. Army's "Army of One" advertising campaign, replacing the long-running and highly successful "Be all you can be." They were attempting to get at the army's heartbeat. But the campaign caused confusion. *Advertising Age's* Bob Garfield called the campaign a "bizarre . . . bait-and-switch." "The Army," he writes, "has never been and will never be about one soldier."

We did our own "Research of One" and asked Scott, a newly turned eighteen-year-old draft registrant, his opinion. He said, "Armies aren't about one anything. I want to go into battle with my team—Jackie Chan, Arnold Schwarzenegger, Jet Li, and me. I get the whole individuality thing they are going for. I really like it, right to the point where I think about the possibility of someone shooting at me. Then I want my team or my mom."

The minds that conceived this campaign tried to connect the multiple symbols of unity, individualism, values, and future with one slogan. They even tried to explain it on the U. S. Army's Web site:

> **Question:** What does "An Army of One" mean?
> **Answer:** The "Army of One" embodies both the strength and unity of the U.S. Army, as well as the physical and mental force inside each and every soldier. It recognizes the individual—the unique talents that soldiers possess. At the same time, it means

the Army is one force with one mission and one set of values. The army is a united team . . . a family. It also discusses the unity between the Active Army, Army National Guard, Army Reserve and veterans, as well as the future's leadership in ROTC and at the U.S. Military Academy.

If you have to work hard to explain a symbol, it's not an effective symbol! The "Army of One" slogan breaks down at the outset, causing rejection rather than connection.

Mixed Messages
We surfed the Internet and found several Web sites that provided us with a list of wonderful mixed metaphors. Below are some of our favorites, including some we invented.

• You've buttered your bread, now lie in it.
• Clearly we have opened a Pandora's box of worms here.
• I've hit the nail on the jackpot.
• He's not playing with a full house.
• It's on the tip of my frontal lobotomy.
• It was so cold last night I had to throw another blanket on the fire.
• It's not rocket surgery.
• I'm shooting from the seat of my pants.
• Rattle some feathers.
• A whole new ball of worms.
• That's a hard bubble to crack.
• That meeting sucked like a train wreck.
• Grasping at the straw that broke the camel's back.
• I'll burn that bridge when I get there.
• Up a tree without a paddle.
• Robbing Peter to pay the piper.
• You smoke like a fish.
• Start at square zero.
• Like ducks on a wire.
• I wouldn't buy this book if you gave it to me.

Sources: Calvin College English Department, <www.calvin.edu/academic/engl/mixmet.htm>; Gary Harris, <www.mixnmangle.com/mix-met>.

Caught in the Act

Saint or sinner, a leader's actions symbolically convey values, vision, and strategy. Gandhi is the quintessential exemplar. He walked to the sea to make salt. He spent an hour a day at a spinning wheel. His goal was neither to manufacture salt, nor weave his own clothes, but to symbolize India's desire to self-govern. Churchill used a parlor trick to symbolize his disagreement. He often pushed a long and straightened paper clip through the center of a cigar. When an adversary took the podium in Parliament, he would light this cigar. All eyes eventually riveted on the growing length of cigar ash, which distracted the politicians from the speaker. Southwest Airlines' Herb Kelleher rode his Harley into a meeting to signify the company's daring spirit. Ted Turner strolled the old CNN newsroom in his bathrobe, exemplifying his eccentric and novel approach to business. Each of these acts added dimension to the story of these leaders.

In Mark Bernstein's great book *Grand Eccentrics: Turning the Century: Dayton and the Inventing of America,* he tells a story about the legendary Charles Kettering. Kettering invented the electric cash register for NCR in 1905, improved automobile ignition systems in 1908, and in 1912 supplied the auto industry's first electric starter for Cadillac through his startup, Delco. By 1919 he was General Motors Corporation's research director, where he developed high-octane, knock-free gasoline, the lightweight two-cycle diesel locomotive engine, and many other important inventions.

Kettering lived in Dayton, Ohio, and commuted to Detroit. He often bragged that he could make the trip in less than four hours, besting all other executives. His secret was to travel side roads that bypassed the traffic-clogged city centers of State Route 25. One day an executive colleague traveled with him and learned the secret. He complained to Kettering, "You aren't taking the normal route." Kettering replied, "You never get anywhere going the obvious way. If you want to get anything done in this world, *get off Route 25.*"

Leaders also use actions to connect to history. First Lady Laura Bush, in a recent address to women CEOs, told them of her experience on the steps of the Texas State Capitol building in Austin. She was there with her mother and others celebrating the seventy-fifth anniversary of women's suffrage. At that moment, she was reflecting on the fact that her mother was a baby when the movement began, and that one of her daughters finds it hard to believe that women were ever denied the right to vote.

Sometimes actions are less dramatic but every bit as effective. We remember a time when a group of busy executives were mandated to attend an all-day leadership development program. Most of them did not want to go, and as we arrived at the off-site conference room, you could see and feel the tension. The session leader had anticipated the resistance. He asked, "How many of you really wish you were not here?" Hands shot up. Some of the faces had that "Can I leave now?" look.

The session leader paused, and then asked, "Have you ever been too busy driving to stop and get gas?" A few laughed, heads nodded, and one executive exclaimed, "Yes, and my car is in the parking lot right now running with the keys locked inside." Everyone laughed, not knowing if he was serious. The laughter reduced the tension and the analogy made the point. The session leader's simple start to a meeting reframed the day for success.

Enduring Symbols

Some symbols seem to last as long as Mother Nature and Father Time. Others have sound bite shelf lives. The 1990 Kodak annual report displayed a white-water rafting trip. The symbolism of "perpetual white water" was not lost on employees and investors. While it worked okay, the white-water symbol lacked the power of originality, as this metaphor was in common usage at the time. In fact, Rogaine also used white-water rapids to explain the perils of hair loss. They produced a video of several balding men bonding on a river raft to help promote their product. Repeated usage during a short time frame may fatigue symbols, eroding their effectiveness. It's like telling a too-familiar joke. Or having only one joke.

Some symbols seem to last as long as Mother Nature and Father Time. Others have sound bite shelf lives.

Using a familiar symbol in a new context, however, can provide fresh meaning. Prior to World War I, a young Captain Douglas MacArthur had to communicate to President Woodrow Wilson his plan to use the National Guard in battle. At that time the Civil War was as fresh in people's minds as the Vietnam War is today. Veterans of the Civil War still marched in parades and spoke to the young guardsmen who served. Each individual state had deep ties to its National Guard units.

Practically speaking, however, the Civil War had been over for fifty years. The states had relaxed their demands on the National Guard, resulting in units that lacked leadership, training, and experience. To remedy this situation, the War Department wanted the National Guard units completely integrated into the regular army. Theirs was a controversial and unpopular proposal.

Captain MacArthur presented a different idea to the White House. He affirmed that the citizen soldiers of the National Guard were an important part of America's democracy. He was against the wholesale integration of the units into the regular army. He proposed creating a division of the army, populated by troops from each state, that would "stretch over the country like a rainbow." Regular army officers would command and train this division and each state would be proudly represented. President Wilson adopted his plan and the great 42nd Rainbow Division was born. They fought with distinction throughout World War I.

Philosophy and Theory

Therefore I speak to them in parables; because they seeing see not; and hearing they hear not, neither do they understand. (Matt. 13:13)

The word *philosophy* has several definitions, including pursuing the love of wisdom, having an affinity for knowledge, and following a thought leader. While philosophy technically includes the disciplines of logic, science, and mathematics, it is more commonly used to describe social, political, existential, and religious views. Philosophic symbols seek to provide understanding, definition, and integration of our emotional, social, and spiritual lives. Philosophies, appealing to emotion and faith, help organize our values and beliefs. Philosophic communication includes stories, parables, myths, rituals, and anthems.

Theories organize and explain our physical universe. Theorists assemble and organize relevant, testable facts, which lead to theories. Theories change as observation tests their validity. These symbolic systems are less about faith and more about proof. Theoretical communication includes mathematical equations, chemical symbols, diagrams, charts, graphs, blueprints, and tables.

Stories Leaders Tell

Do you struggle to memorize a phone number, yet remember the details of stories you heard years ago? Right now, without looking, recite your company's values. Okay, now start singing any one of the dozens of songs from your days as a teenager. Can you recount a favorite fairy tale, movie scene, or novel? After a meeting ends and the speeches are finished, what do you remember? *The stories.* Your mind is designed to collect and remember stories. The mind retains what is vividly imagined as well as what is vividly experienced.

"Telling stories, in the sense of registering what happens in the form of brain maps, is probably a brain obsession," writes Dr. Antonio Damasio, "and probably begins relatively early both in terms of evolution and in terms of the complexity of the neural structures required to create narratives. Telling stories precedes language, since it is, in fact, a condition for language, and it is based not just in the cerebral cortex but elsewhere in the brain and in the right hemisphere as well as the left."

Stories explain the unexplainable. Every culture has used stories to explain such mysteries as why the sun comes up each morning, why the weather changes, how the gods became gods, and where mothers go when they die. Myth, tradition, morality, and religious stories teach children complexities in ways they can understand. Neurologist Oliver Sacks wrote, "It is this narrative or symbolic power which gives a sense of the world—a concrete reality in the imaginative form of symbol and story—when abstract thought can provide nothing at all. A child follows the Bible before he follows Euclid. Not because the Bible is simpler (the reverse might be said), but because it is cast in a symbolic and narrative mode."

Stories that are not necessarily true on the outside but perfectly true on the inside are called *parables*. They communicate across all three channels in unison, engaging the whole brain. Well-constructed and well-delivered stories are captivating and memorable because they include details, dialogue, and drama.

Marilyn Carlson Nelson is the chairman and CEO of Carlson Companies, Inc., owning such brands as Radisson Hotels, Radisson Seven Seas Cruises, T.G.I. Friday's, and Carlson Travel. Marilyn was speaking at a diversity conference at the College of St. Benedict, a women's college in St. Joseph, Minnesota, and wanted to make a point about the importance of personal responsibility, initiative, and resolve. She chose to tell a personal story:

. . . What I'm talking about really is personal accountability. I learned a lot about it at a tender age.

When I was a little girl, my family was on our way home from church one Sunday, and I was really upset because I felt Sunday school, which I was attending at the time, was a total disaster. I mean it was a total disaster—the boys were throwing spitballs, etc. So I announced to my parents that I wanted to stop going to Sunday school and instead go to the sanctuary to hear the sermon with the adults.

I suppose I thought that they'd think it was pretty good that I was so mature, and that I wanted to hear the sermon rather than go to Sunday school. Instead, my dad was furious, got very upset with me and said, "Well, of course you'll keep going to Sunday school."

I protested and said, "But I'd get more out of the sermon."

And he said, "If you don't like Sunday school, then change it."

Well, I was probably eleven at the time and we attended a huge, downtown church in Minneapolis, and here was my father telling me to fix Sunday school. Well, yeah, sure Dad.

My mom tried to rescue me and said, "Oh, Curt, that's unreasonable." But then he got mad at my mother! The long and short of it is that my dad always got his way and knowing I wasn't going to win, I started to cry.

That didn't do any good. When we got home, he sent me to my room and I had to come downstairs later with a list of all the things that I thought were wrong with the Sunday school and all the ways I thought it could be fixed.

Then my mother had to get the number of the Sunday school superintendent, and I had to call him to make an appointment. Can't you imagine how I thought it would go? "Oh hi, this is Marilyn Carlson and you know, I'm in the sixth grade, and I have a few suggestions to fix Sunday school." As you can imagine, I thought it would go over really big.

In the end, the superintendent said, "Actually we've been worried about the Sunday school, and we would really appreciate your ideas."

So, sure enough, my mother, who always seemed to somehow get involved in the punishment for my sins, had to drive me downtown to the church in the middle of the week. We had a meeting, got other kids involved, and we fixed the Sunday school!

Carlson Companies was named one of the "100 Best Companies to Work for in America" by *Fortune* in its February 4, 2002, edition. *Working Woman* magazine named the organization one of the one hundred best companies for working mothers.

3-D Storytelling: Details, Dialogue, and Drama

During a meeting with Jody Lewis, a Valvoline executive, the phone rang. Her three-year-old, Conner, was looking for his laptop. Jody told Conner to talk to his father. After the call, Jody explained that she and her husband were withholding Conner's laptop as part of his toilet training.

Here's how this incident becomes a story through injecting details, dialogue, and drama. This story is an effective metaphor for both fast-changing technology and the power of "Generation Next." Boyd tells the story this way:

> Jody Lewis is an energetic, talented young executive at the retail division of Ashland Oil, known as Valvoline Instant Oil Change, or VIOC. During an intense planning session in her office, the private line on her phone rang and in a reflex motion she pressed the speakerphone button, "This is Jody."
>
> "Mommy," said the sweet little voice, "Mommy, where is my laptop?" This was a call from her three-year-old son, Conner. Having four children of my own, I smiled at Jody and listened in on a wonderful conversation.
>
> "Hi, honey," she said.
>
> "Mommy, I can't find my laptop."
>
> "Conner, go find your daddy, and he will tell you how to get your computer. OK?"
>
> "OK, Mommy. But I want my laptop."
>
> "I know you do, honey. Go find your daddy and talk to him. Bye-bye. I'll see you at home in a little while. I love you, Conner."
>
> Conner's father is a financial consultant who telecommutes

from their Lexington, Kentucky, home. I thought how cute it was that Conner couldn't find his little Fisher-Price or Speak and Spell computer. No, it's a full-blown IBM ThinkPad. Conner was using it to learn colors, numbers, and words, as well as play some cool games.

Jody further explained to me that the previous night they had had a family meeting. They explained to Conner he could not use his laptop until he learned to use THE BIG POTTY. This little kid isn't potty trained, but he does just fine with his own ThinkPad, thank you very much.

Boyd then shows a photograph of Conner at his computer, with a caption, "Meet your competition."

Many of your personal experiences can become useful stories by simply adding details, dialogue, and drama.

We hope you become skilled at all forms of symbolism, but learning to tell a story is mandatory. Storytelling, like business analysis, is an art form that improves with practice.

The Sound of Silos

Chapter Seven

Themes create communication threads . . .

Communication is beautifully simple and excruciatingly complex. We communicate in facts, emotions, and symbols, yet there is more. This chapter is about three important dynamics of communication connections. We call them levels, quadrants, and themes. To make connections, leaders must communicate with facts, emotions, and symbols on a variety of levels, from the trivial to the personal. They must know when to communicate in public and when to communicate in private. And they also must know the importance of incorporating a few simple themes into their communication. Leaders who say everything say nothing.

Dive! Dive! Dive!

No doubt you have passed someone in the hallway and said, "Hello," to hear that person respond, "Fine." This disconnected exchange illustrates the first level of communication. Social communication is like clothing. It conveys easy-to-decipher information about identity, lifestyle, or attitude that is not particularly important or personal. Like clothing, social communication is transitory, automatic, and changes at the rate of fashion. British anthropologist Robin Dunbar is an expert on primate communication. His intriguing, data-rich theories suggest that human primates groom each other through social communication. Gossip, weather updates, headline news, what's for dinner, and the latest scores are necessary surface chatter. E-mail grants distant neighbors a chance to chat over a "cyber-fence." If it weren't for humans' need for social communication, e-mail may never have been so quickly adopted.

It is exhausting to always talk about important or complicated matters. Trivial or tantalizing conversation helps people find common ground, explore similar interests, and maintain social connections. Have you ever talked to someone seated next to you on an airplane or train, exchanged funny, even semi-important stories about your children, and yet never exchanged names? Have you ever had lively conversations in an online chat room, knowing none of the real identities?

At the *significant* communication level, we slip below fashion to more important issues. We talk about priorities, relationships, problem solving, and goals. If you have ever debated politics or profits, religion or business strategy, then you know communication can become important and personal. Constituents will align behind leaders who state clearly what they deeply feel and believe. We also expect our leaders to help us discuss the pressing and complex issues we face but often avoid. Georgianne Smith used our leadership communication model in a public forum to conduct research for her master's thesis about leadership communication. She found that empathy and inspiration are communicated when a leader "accurately interprets my feelings," "understands me," and "seems aligned with my opinions and beliefs."

Intimate communication is the deepest level. Usually reserved for spouses, close allies, and deities, it conveys those fears and aspirations we are reluctant to reveal publicly. It is characterized by openness, high trust, and vulnerability. On occasion, leaders, even in public, declare personal beliefs or open up to a degree that feels close to intimate conversation. More often, however, this level of communication is reserved for very small groups.

Leaders transition from social to significant, even to intimate, and back again. They use facts, emotions, and symbols to help constituents make the transition between each level.

Social   Significant   Intimate

As we describe these three major communication levels we realize that, like human emotions, they have an infinite variety of shades. Bob Galvin, son of Motorola's founder, Paul Galvin, and father of the current CEO, Chris Galvin, was an admired, trusted, and beloved leader during his tenure as CEO. Galvin's constituents remember him for a great many things, including his personal touch. As we've worked with executives from Motorola over the years, we have heard a lot of stories about Galvin, like this one:

> I was asked to meet Mr. Galvin at the airport and take him to his hotel. As we drove, he asked how I thought the company was doing. Shocking as it may seem, I told the CEO the truth. Presuming I was competent and had something to contribute, he asked me about my job and what I needed to do it better. He asked me about my family, and we talked about what was important to each of us in our careers and lives. He sent me a personal note a few days later, thanking me for giving him a ride and for speaking with him candidly about our work.

In his communication, Bob Galvin consistently connected at deeper levels than most leaders ever do. Many leaders do not want to communicate at deeper levels. Somehow it feels too uncomfortable, too time-consuming, and just too hard. If you want to connect with an individual or group at deeper levels, take the plunge. Asking questions and then listening is a good starting point.

Movies often dramatize how leaders move us to deeper levels of communication. Portraying Lieutenant Commander Ron Hunter in the 1995 movie *Crimson Tide*, actor Denzel Washington is in a power struggle with Captain Frank Ramsey, played by Gene Hackman. They are aboard the USS *Alabama* as the submarine prepares to fire its nuclear missiles on Russia to prevent a renegade general from firing on the United States. Hunter has made the gut-wrenching decision to mutiny against his trigger-happy captain.

Toward the end of the movie, the USS

The Three Levels of Communication

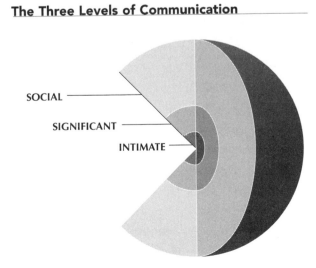

SOCIAL

SIGNIFICANT

INTIMATE

Alabama is under attack by a Russian sub, and the only radio that can confirm whether they should launch nuclear missiles is broken. Attempting to solve this critical problem, a desperate Hunter goes down to the radio room to talk directly with Petty Officer Russell Vossler. Hunter encounters an overwhelmed sailor surrounded by wrecked radio equipment.

"Do you know what's going on here?" asks Commander Hunter. Vossler, disoriented, weakly answers, "Yes, sir."

Hunter doesn't believe that the distraught crewman truly understands or is able to act. Needing to get through to him, Hunter speaks the facts to Vossler in a confidential and urgent manner.

"No, I don't think you do. Let me explain it to you. If we launch and we're wrong, what's left of Russia is going to launch at us. There will be a nuclear Holocaust beyond imagination. So, it's all about knowing, Mr. Vossler. We have to know whether or not our order to launch has been recalled or not. The only way we are going to know is if you fix that radio. Do you understand?"

Vossler's mouth says yes, but his eyes and body language are still saying *no*. Realizing that the gravity of the situation is not sinking in with the fraught radio operator, Hunter tries communicating with symbols at the social level.

"Do you ever watch *Star Trek*?" he asks Vossler. "You know. *Star Trek*. The USS *Enterprise*?"

Vossler's eyes pop open with interest and comprehension. "Remember when the Klingons were going to blow up the *Enterprise*," Hunter continues, "and Captain Kirk calls down to Scotty. And he says, 'Scotty, I've got to have more power.'"

"He needs more warp speed!" Vossler blurts.

Having gained his attention, Hunter pulls the metaphor back down to the *significant* level. "I'm Captain Kirk. You're Scotty. I need more power."

Seeing that Vossler is beginning to comprehend the situation, Hunter deepens his inflection, pulls closer, and emphasizes with *significant* emotion, "I'm telling you. If you do not get this radio up, a billion people are going to die. Now, it's all up to you. Can you handle it, Scotty?"

"Aye, Captain," Vossler responds.

Public and Private Communication

Leaders communicate publicly and privately. They decide when an e-mail will suffice or when a handwritten note is the nicer touch. They decide when

The Four Quadrants of Communication

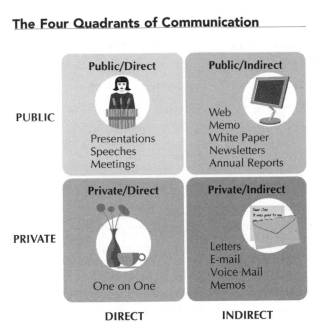

	DIRECT	INDIRECT
PUBLIC	**Public/Direct** Presentations Speeches Meetings	**Public/Indirect** Web Memo White Paper Newsletters Annual Reports
PRIVATE	**Private/Direct** One on One	**Private/Indirect** Letters E-mail Voice Mail Memos

to call, when to walk down the hallway, or when to fly across the country to comfort a wounded employee or needy client.

The distinction between the two is not always simple, but for simplicity's sake we will refer to private communication as one-on-one and public communication as one-to-many. Leaders also communicate in immediate and delayed time frames. Direct communication allows for immediate reaction or conversation, whether the communication is face-to-face or via technology such as teleconference or videoconference. Voice mail, e-mail, and handwritten communication are forms of indirect communication. The response time is delayed.

Speaking before a group is a public/direct event. This communication is real-time, face-to-face, with the opportunity for immediate response by constituents. When a leader sends out an e-mail or voice mail to an individual, he or she is communicating from the private/indirect quadrant. This communication is one-on-one, not face-to-face, and has a delayed response.

When we communicate dissimilar messages in different quadrants, then the lie detector needles spike and communication is filtered and questioned. For example, suppose an eloquent and convincing leader speaks well publicly about relationships, community, and collaboration. Yet during private conversations he seldom mentions those same concepts and instead gossips incessantly. Most would conclude that his public face is a political façade, a premeditated act, or a calculating counterfeit. Even if it is genuine, only those very close to him can resolve the apparent contradiction.

We have illustrated the factual, emotional, and symbolic principles primarily with public communication examples. However, the indirect quadrants are the greatest challenges for many leaders. For many of us, e-mail is like an electronic repetitive-motion injury. There appears to be no universal salve for this electronic strain. Yet it would also seem like a major step backward to eliminate instant messaging and e-mail capabilities.

We are like social infants with massive communication power. We sit in the middle of a worldwide virtual living room, shouting for everyone to pay attention. Our very human tendency toward social communication has collided with instant messaging, and e-mail glut is the result. Yet we simultaneously complain and brag about the quantity of e-mail we receive.

As part of an archaic "CYA" survival strategy, many people strangle the electronic communication network by habitually overusing e-mail. Every minuscule decision or iota of information is copied to the world. People often say, "Got to go. I've got a hundred e-mails waiting for me." No matter that half of them merely involve the latest company joke or office birthday party. It's a ridiculous onslaught.

"There is no organization chart that matters at Sun," touted John Gage of Sun Microsystems. "What matters is e-mail traffic." This game of e-mail envy may make us feel important, but the challenge for the leader is to use this technology to create meaning instead of quantity. While The Leader's Voice cannot stop the deluge, it can help your messages gain greater emphasis and help raise the e-mail communication in your organization to a more important level. E-mail is important and can be an effective communication tool.

While Denzel's Lieutenant Commander Hunter is fictional, Alec Fraser is not. A U.S. Naval Academy graduate, Fraser spent twenty-four years in the United States Navy, serving as a ship captain on destroyers and cruisers. His last command, USS *Cape St. George* (CG 71), earned the Arizona Memorial Trophy for being the most combat-ready ship in both the Atlantic and Pacific Fleets.

Today, Fraser is president of Turner Properties. In effect, he is the landlord for CNN, Cartoon Network, TBS Superstation, TNT, Turner Classic Movies, and the other companies of Turner Broadcasting. His 480 employees handle everything from changing lightbulbs to managing the construction of the new street-level CNN studio in New York City. They handle security, parking, air conditioning, remodeling, and multimillion-dollar construction budgets. Their job is the safety, health, and comfort of over ten thousand people who work for Turner Broadcasting all over the world.

"On my ship," he told us in an interview, referring to his navy days, "I focused on formal and informal communication." The formal communication consisted mostly of written memos, policy standards, and standing orders. Fraser's number one standing order: "No Brussels sprouts." However, Fraser said the main purpose of formal communication was to be clear about "when you shoot and when you don't."

"The captain can't be everywhere," he said, "so you really need to spend a lot of time communicating potential threats and changes in the orders." For Fraser, informal communication consisted of simply "picking up the microphone from the bridge and speaking plainly." Fraser is a great believer in the "just let everyone know what's going on" leadership communication philosophy. His terms "formal" and "informal" describe the ability to move through the levels of communication in both the public and private quadrants. While his communiqué on Brussels sprouts was *social,* it was public/indirect. Fraser's conversations from the bridge were public/direct and shifted between *social* and *significant.*

His navy experience was especially useful after September 11, 2001. "I went back into captain mode," he said. Located across the street from downtown Atlanta's Centennial Olympic Park, The CNN Center is a public building with a food court, retail stores, and a hotel, in addition to offices. Railroad tracks run underneath the building. More than three million people annually pass through the center. Each year, the CNN Studio Tour offers more than three hundred thousand guests a behind-the-scenes look at CNN's news operations. In terms only a former military commander would use, Fraser describes The CNN Center as "terrible ground to defend." With CNN being recognized as the world's news leader, he had to consider the company's prime real estate as a potential target.

So, Fraser immediately beefed up security, shut down the CNN Studio Tour, installed tire spikes on the train tracks to keep cars from using the rail lines, and instituted a myriad of other security precautions. At the same time, he relied on e-mail to communicate to the ten thousand-plus Turner Broadcasting employees "what was going on." "While the e-mail was formal, I tried to keep the language informal."

As the news of anthrax letters at NBC and other media companies reached CNN, Fraser immediately moved all mail into trailers across the street. He again turned to e-mail. Fraser's e-mail dated October 23, 2001, begins, "I wanted to take a few minutes to brief you on the measures we are taking . . ." His e-mail then explains some of the new procedures for employees. "The revised mail-handling processes implemented this week are working well." In a straightforward sentence that reveals how much things changed after September 11, Fraser writes, "Gloves and masks have been distributed to all locations so employees who so desire can wear them when opening mail."

Naturally, some employees were a bit nervous about walking across the street into a trailer full of mail. To allay fears, Fraser continued his weekly e-mails updating employees about security measures. He also worked in the trailers opening mail along with Turner's chairman and CEO Jamie Kellner. To calm nerves, he had his staff add a velvet Elvis painting on the wall of the trailer and pink flamingo lawn decorations on the outside. "We wanted the trailers to feel like trailers." With tire spikes, flamingos, and e-mails, Alec Fraser communicated in multiple quadrants and at multiple levels. Something every executive should learn.

Themes: Communication Building Blocks

Leaders connect with their constituents using a few key themes. Themes often define the common ground between a leader's ideology and the long-standing corporate ideology. They express themselves in values, brand attributes, imperatives, and philosophy. Themes are key ideas or principles that support and reveal the leader's agenda and intentions. Themes connect people to important ideas and create deeper levels of dialogue.

Themes as a leadership communication strategy initially grabbed our attention as we studied political leaders like Churchill, Thatcher, Gandhi, Kohemeni, Ho Chi Minh, Mao Tse-tung, Reagan, Roosevelt, Meir, Kennedy, and Corazon Aquino. These leaders continually stressed, sometimes with poetic cadence, a few central principles or ideas. Themes worked as bullet points for their long-term agenda and were not merely pep rally slogans. They used facts, emotions, and symbols to ensure the themes were understood, agreed upon, cared about, and acted on. The themes connected the simple with the complex, the trivial with the urgent, and the timely with the timeless.

Most business professionals are familiar with former General Electric CEO Jack Welch's "boundary-less organization" and Intel chairman Andy

Grove's "paranoia." Both leaders used their respective themes successfully over long time periods. We found that effective communicators used the same technique. Timothy J. McKibben, chairman of Ancor Holdings in Dallas, Texas, keeps a group of high-growth companies bound together by constantly preaching "creativity, cooperation, and self-improvement."

Themes create communication threads that tie nodes on the network together. They invite individuals to voice their opinions. You can tell if a theme has struck home if constituents want to discuss and debate its relevance and merit. Themes allow the new leader to place his or her personal stamp on the long-standing company ideals, values, or identity. As we write, Bob Lutz at General Motors is trying to reestablish the frayed and broken theme of "great design." It has sparked debate and excitement.

Leadership Themes

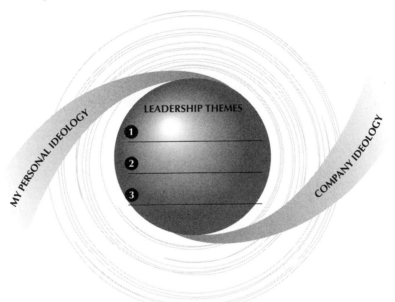

Jack Rouse is founder and CEO of Jack Rouse Associates. Jack designs theme parks for a living. Before that, he was a professor of opera and musical theater. Universal Studios, LEGOLAND, Warner Brothers, Cirque du Soleil, Volkswagen, and dozens of other companies have turned to him for advice on creating "themed experiences." However, Jack believes that a theme is not a story: "Shakespeare wrote to themes of love and revenge. The theme may set the stage, but the story delivers the message."

So, if customer service is one of your themes, you still have to tell the customer story.

Nodes on the Network

Human beings congregate. We create tribes, teams, communities, and nations. The same natural dynamics that bind us together also serve to insulate us from other groups, creating silos. Creating team identity unites the group, but also creates a set of conditions for membership. These conditions can become so strong that they insulate the group from others, causing a variety of communication problems among network nodes. Research and our experience suggest there are predictable shifts in group dynamics when groups reach sizes of approximately three, eight, twelve, and thirty-three. Each of these groups can become a silo.

Dunbar's data shows that from tribal communities to the modern military, informal allegiance occurs naturally. He further explains that informal communication patterns cannot be maintained in a group beyond a population of 150. This happens because human brain capacity to juggle informal social relationships reaches maximum potential at this point. Maintaining cohesion after this level, let alone allegiance, requires a formal system that often includes rules, regulations, and rank.

In the military, the maximum size of a functional unit rarely exceeds 200 and is regularly limited to around 100. On the real *Ohio*-class ballistic missile submarine USS *Alabama*, there is a crew compliment of 15 officers and 140 enlisted. This seems to be a limit all military leaders have discovered and rediscovered over the centuries. Even the Romans had a basic unit of 100, headed by a centurion.

Bill Gore is the late founder of W. L. Gore & Associates, a high-tech organization specializing in fibers, fabrics, and related products. While he's probably better known in the world for the invention of GORE-TEX, we think his thoughts on organizational behavior are more important. He found that groups' production and innovation declined after reaching 150 people, so he kept plant populations in his company at or below this number. Following a "flat lattice" style of organization, Gore & Associates does not use titles, and "sponsors" have replaced "bosses." A group with less than 150 can create and maintain a functioning work group in which everyone can know everyone else through informal social connections.

Our virtual, networked world has stressed our natural capacity to communicate informally. Maintaining allegiance by wire and wireless technologies for groups of 150 and more is proving to be very difficult. The people of this world evolved by learning to live together. Frequent face-to-face contact with the others maintains connection and trust. On the other hand, e-mail, teleconference, and voice mail place stress on leaders' ability to connect with constituents and their ability to connect with each other.

> **Frequent face-to-face contact with others maintains connection and trust ... e-mail, teleconference, and voice mail place stress on leaders' ability to connect with constituents and their ability to connect with each other.**

These dynamics are part of what we believe is causing the leadership communication crisis. This noisy, new, networked world requires leaders to have a more powerful and eloquent voice or they will become commanders who submarine their own silos.

Attention and Interest

Leaders have to earn the right to be heard. Like everyone else, leaders compete in the marketplace of time and ideas for constituents' *attention* and *interest*. Silos are only one of a thousand natural roadblocks to effective communication. Cynicism, mistrust, and skepticism can result in your messages being filtered, or even dismissed. The more message-rich the environment, the tougher it is to compete.

Many leaders unwittingly and unknowingly camouflage their communication, inadvertently blending it with the mountains of meaningless chatter. A close look at the dynamics of attention can help us compete. Things that attract our attention have specific qualities including, intensity, repetition, striking quality, and definiteness of form. The intensity of one blue marble in a hundred white ones draws our attention. Harry Quadracci, CEO of Quad/Graphics says, "The leader's job is to say the same thing over and over again in different ways." The unique and quiet voice may be heard above a thousand clamoring ones. Gaining attention or maintaining interest is increased when one or more of these features are used. In fact, the science of camouflage reveals that diluting intensity, disrupting repetitive patterns, removing striking quality, and blurring sharp outlines cause an object (or message) to disappear against the background.

Cliff Bartow succeeded Dave Brown as CEO of LensCrafters, now part of Luxottica Retail Group. We interviewed a group of company managers, asking about Cliff's communication effectiveness. They said he had captured the company's attention with his goals and agenda. "Our department knows exactly what the company wants." We thought they might be exaggerating, so we asked them what the exact goals were. The group recited them in unison.

We traced the beginning of this clarity back to a single January leadership meeting. Cliff had three specific goals for the year, each with a metric. The goals were to attain a precise level of operating income, to achieve an increased level of customer satisfaction, and to attain a certain position on *Fortune*'s "Best Places to Work" list. Repeated time and again, these metrics became mantras for everyone. LensCrafters attained two of the three and set up similarly clear goals the following year.

What gains our attention does not necessarily hold our interest. Now that you have constituents' attention, how do you maintain their interest? Novelty, importance, suspense, conflict, animation, familiarity, and humor are the characteristics of interesting communication. Themes work because they naturally have many of the qualities required for attention and interest. The principles of attention and interest apply at all levels and quadrants of communication.

The facts you use must be clear, relevant, and compelling; the emotions, rich, intense, and heartfelt; the symbols, memorable and meaningful. But before you can win their hearts and minds, you must first get their attention and then keep their interest.

Without
Wax

Chapter Eight

As a leader, you are irrelevant until you have something to say.

I n ancient Rome, statuary was the ultimate status symbol, representing wealth, importance, and even immortality. Sculptors, revered and rewarded, became skilled with stone and wax. Yes, we said *wax*. Scars from a misguided chisel or natural flaws in the stone were skillfully filled with colored wax. The wax disguised such imperfections until the sun, wind, or time revealed the flaw.

The most sought-after artisans refused this practice and proudly displayed a *Sine Cera* sign on their shop doors. The Latin term *sine cera* means "without wax." The sculptors who worked *sine cera* guaranteed the real thing. In today's terms, they were *sincere*.

How many leaders would be willing to place this sign on their personal Web site? *Sine cera* leaders are unpretentious. Wax free, they do not pretend to be someone they are not or to feel something they do not. They are honest and real. They know who they are and aren't afraid to show it. Unfortunately, too many leaders attempt to cover their flaws, their true feelings, or the truth with a form of wax.

Psychologist Abraham Maslow observed that "Authentic self-hood is being able to hear these impulse voices within oneself: To know what one really wants or doesn't want, what one is fit for and what one is not fit for... finding what your true self is and wants and in that process discovering your ability to lead."

Iain Morris is *sine cera*. Iain was a middle manager with Motorola's Paging Products Group. Several years ago, the company had invited us to work with his engineering group responsible for new designs. At the time, the marketplace was exploding with demand for new pagers. They were immersed in the

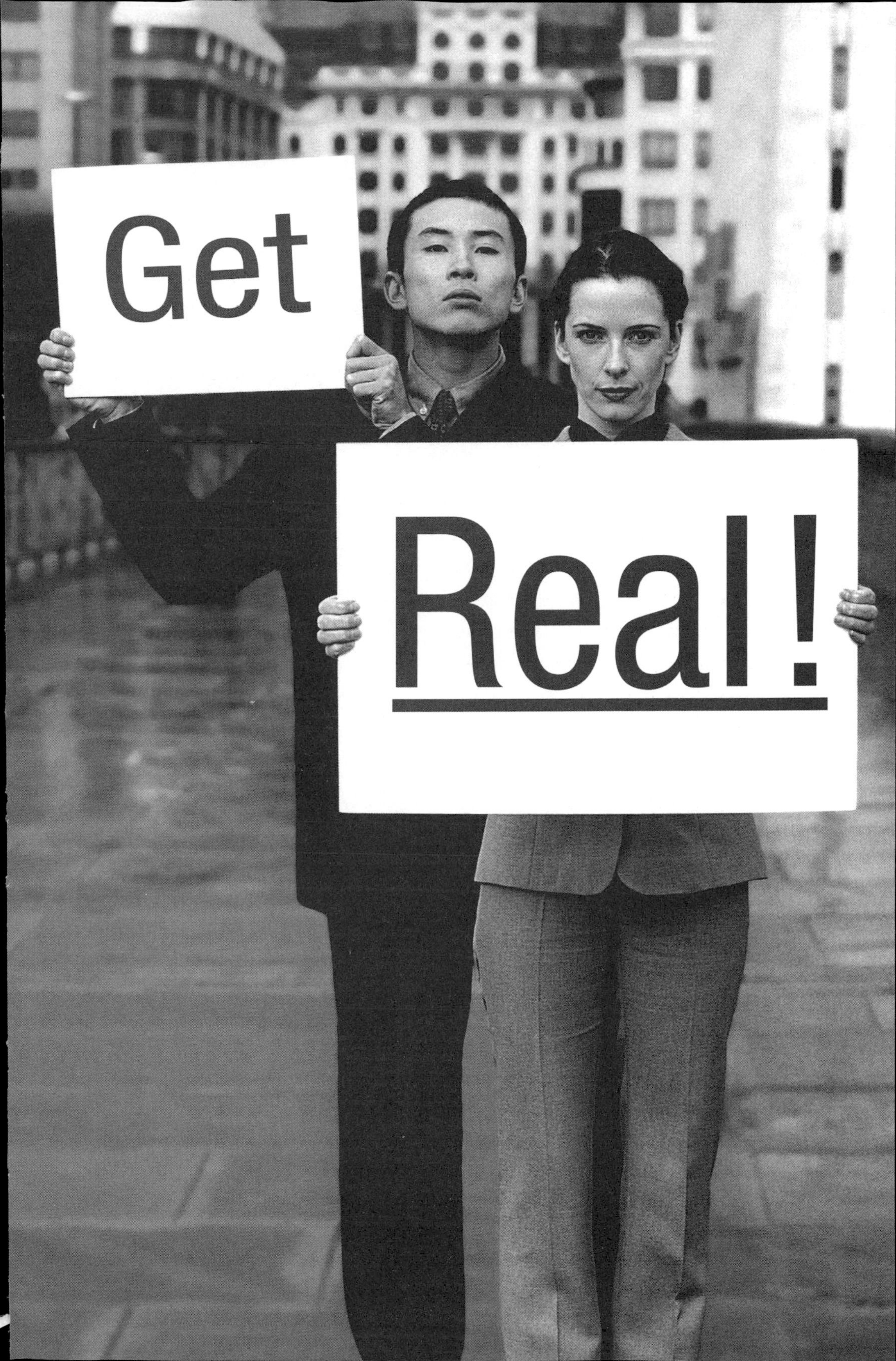
Get
Real!

new-product-cycle pressure cooker. We were present when Iain, the senior manager of the group, kicked off a two-day meeting.

Iain arrived with a sheaf of dog-eared papers, apparently preparing to read his script aloud. The power of his communication that night, in our experience, has rarely been matched. Iain looked at his notes twice as he started speaking, then laying them aside he continued passionately and earnestly for fifteen minutes, relating his deepest beliefs about leadership. He used imagery like celebrity chef Emeril uses spices. He declared that leaders were "not experts, but brokers" of skilled talent. He challenged his engineers with a Renaissance metaphor, "On a Michelangelo scale of one to ten, we are somewhat further down the scale." He was telling his group that their creative genius needed to kick into gear or they would lose in the marketplace. To him, a best-in-class circuit design was a work of art. He expressed his belief in his group and their ability to win, finishing to hearty applause.

While Iain can deliver a polished speech and use skillful rhetoric when the occasion calls for it, he prefers to keep the imagery simple and his message straightforward when motivating groups. This particular night the conviction in his voice spoke volumes. He told us he believed the only way a manager should communicate with his team was to "tell it straight, simple, and with enthusiasm." A team member told us, "Iain doesn't need a circuit schematic to tell us what is important to him. He lives this leadership stuff every day. That's why we admire him. He feels so strongly about our work and us. Iain is, well, simply Iain."

Effective leadership communication is without wax. It occurs when followers hear from the real person. We trust, admire, and follow authentic people because we long to be authentic ourselves. As role models, leaders are often symbols of our better selves—people we aspire to be like. We loathe phoniness and crave genuine leaders who truly stand for something, who believe in something.

Hucksters tell great stories. Leaders tell *their* stories.

Hucksters tell great stories. Leaders tell *their* stories. The search for one's voice is simply the search for self. Often leaders don't know what they want to say, because they don't know who they are. If your only intention is to sell someone, then any story might do. If you want to sell yourself as a leader, you have to tell your story. The leader's message grows naturally from a clear sense of self.

Self-Mastery

At the end of a daylong lecture, we asked business philosopher Peter Koestenbaum, "So, Peter, what is the meaning of life?"

He answered without hesitation, "It is to become mature."

"Exactly what do you mean, mature?"

Holding up a clenched fist, he said, "Mature people have a strong sense of self. They know who they are, what they believe in, confident in their opinions and judgment." He held up his other hand in an open, relaxed gesture. "They also have a humility that helps them continue to listen and learn, they care about other human beings, and are willing to serve. When you are both of these at the same time, you are mature." While not all authentic people are mature, all mature people are authentic. Have you ever worked for a jerk? Have you ever been a jerk? Jerks can be authentic, but never mature.

Ultimately, those who fail to be authentic fail to achieve their possible greatness and often self-destruct. "A man has two great levers on his soul," said Napoleon Bonaparte, "inspiration and fear." Inspiration is the thrust and lift that moves leaders toward a more authentic life. Fear is the weight and drag that pulls them down. We soar toward self-mastery if inspiration is strong and dive toward self-destruction if fear rules.

The Desire to Lead

The aspiration to achieve something worthy or significant is common among the most common of people. Clergy, philosophers, psychiatrists, and scientists are often asked, "What is the meaning of life?" The real question is "What's the meaning of *my* life?" Leo Tolstoy wrote in a letter to his intended fiancée, Valery Arsenev, that the purpose of a worthy life was "to work for the person one loves and to love one's work." Tolstoy's sentiment predated the same conclusion reached by Freud and by Viktor Frankl, a Holocaust survivor and author of *Man's Search for Meaning*.

A person's identity can only rise above the trivial if they aspire to accomplish things that matter. Our aims must have some significance, else we are

The Authenticity Model

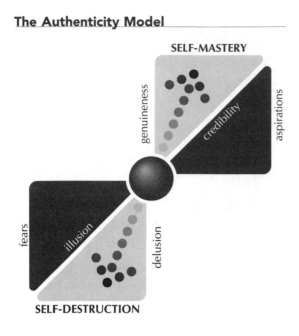

SELF-MASTERY

genuineness

credibility

aspirations

fears

illusion

delusion

SELF-DESTRUCTION

doomed to continually ask, "Is this all there is?" Koestenbaum argues that personal distinction is the direct result of a good leadership strategy colliding with authentic development.

Leading often promotes accelerated emotional maturation. It can also lead to self-destruction. The person who leads will hear power's seductive call and daily confront the need to remain credible.

Leadership invites us to confront our fears, our flaws, our beliefs about authority, and the quality of our relationships. Leaders are buffeted by undeserved criticism, lulled by unearned praise, and frustrated by the difficulty of getting things done through the efforts of others.

Genuine or Counterfeit?

"I think somehow, we learn who we really are and then live with that decision," said Eleanor Roosevelt. Her comment seems to strike at the heart of the maturation process. Coming to grips with oneself is a lifelong effort. Knowing yourself, living with that knowledge, and disclosing it without defense, camouflage, or pretense is the essence of authenticity. As psychologist and management consultant Manfred Kets de Vries has observed, "A good sense of identity allows a person to feel good in their skin."

A colleague, with a historically strong need to be liked, describes waking up one morning shortly after his fortieth birthday and just not caring as much about what other people thought of him. He describes a profoundly liberating feeling of being free to be himself. As we relinquish the quest for who we think we should be and discover who we actually are, genuineness and vulnerability emerge as new and comfortable friends. Psychologist Carl Rogers observed, "The curious paradox is that when I accept myself just as

I am, then I can change." The key to transforming our organizations and ourselves is to stop pretending that they are what they are not. Embrace the uncomfortable truth.

Leaders who are authentic, who remain true to who they are and what they believe, retain their follower's ear. When trust is high, communication bypasses all the natural filters that protect us from being cheated and deceived. With barriers down and filters removed, a few authentic words can speak volumes.

When you hide behind a façade, stay safe, or keep your emotional distance, others—not knowing who you really are—filter what you say to keep themselves safe. The reverberating cry for more communication often expresses the need of constituents to connect with those leaders who remain distant. In some cases, more communication actually makes things worse. When leaders are not trusted and they communicate more, it simply provides the organization with more things not to believe. The cry for more communication is often the symptom of the undiagnosed disease, mistrust. The disease is cured with authentic communication, not more communication.

Psychologists know that most people enter into trust with relative ease, but some find trust difficult. Most groups are comprised of people representing both of these characteristics. Psychologists refer to those willing to trust as "high-trusters" and those wary of trust as "low-trusters." When leaders communicate competitive messages, the willing tend to be okay, but the trust level for the wary goes down. Cooperative messages increase the level of trust among the willing. In this case, the wary's trust does not decrease, which is as good as it gets for them. Inconsistent messages cause trust to plummet for both the willing and the wary. Cooperative and consistent messages secure the greatest level of trust.

Taking Stock

"Your stock just went up" means you are more trusted. Like stock, we evaluate multiple indicators to determine an overall trust value for others. Three important indicators are morality, intentions, and competence. In most of the relationships in our lives, morality and intentions are the prime indicators. In business, competence assumes equal status and is often the leading indicator. Competence is expressed both in our technical ability and interpersonal ability. A leader's stock rises and falls dramatically based on the ability to communicate, because it is linked directly to our willingness to trust. We evaluate both message and messenger; therefore, voice and trust are inseparably linked.

The Ability to Be Believed

Credibility is defined as "the condition of being believable." It is linked with reputation, status, and legitimacy. The word itself comes from two words, *credo*, meaning, "I believe," and *ability*. The word *credo* is the root word for credentials, creed, and credit.

As leaders we do not grow in isolation. Who we are and what we believe are shaped through our conversations and interactions with others. Important people influence us more. A little bit of each of them becomes part of us. The height of authenticity occurs when we integrate these voices into that single voice, uniquely ours, inseparably linked with a unique self-image. As we mature we learn to speak with a clarity that captures the attention of others.

Authenticity further demands the integration of voice and behavior. Our ability to "walk our talk" begins with our beliefs. When we choose to lead, our voice and actions speak our intentions. As news executive Roger Ailes wrote, "The world has changed. So has the way we communicate. Those who fail to adopt will be left behind. But for those who want to succeed there is only one secret: You are the message."

Fear and Loathing in Leadership

Why do human beings try to hide who they are and what they believe? Unhealthy fear is a prime reason—not the rational fear of impending physical danger, but the irrational fears that plague us all at some time. Fear of confrontation or self-revelation can diminish confidence, motivation, the ability to acquire and maintain relationships, and the ability to lead. Many commonly shared and rather ordinary fears exist that shape our anxieties. These fears are pervasive across cultures and time but are regularly mastered by those willing to confront them. We are afraid of looking bad, being judged, being found out, being rejected, and simply not being liked. Fear is the slave master of deception. Unhealthy needs are fear's partners in self-destruction. We need to be liked, gain control, have power, possess wealth, look perfect, be famous, or command admiration. These needs and fears create resistance to maturity, perhaps tracing back to childhood trauma or other psychodynamic origins. Some people fail to mature because of limiting beliefs about themselves, relationships, religion, politics, or marriage.

Fear doesn't work. Try courage.

Pop quiz: Which of these needs, which of these fears cause you to misrepresent yourself? What about yourself do you deliberately hide from others? Who do you deceive and why?

What do you fear?

Acceptable Flaws

In the heat of crisis or with the gentle sustained pressure of time, hidden flaws are revealed and the leader loses trust, along with goodwill and loyalty. No one expects you to be the perfect role model, but they do expect to see a close connection between who you profess to be and who you really are.

People are even willing to look past the acceptable flaws of an authentic leader. Flaws make us human, more accessible, even more endearing, and within reasonable boundaries, we readily forgive and even embrace some flaws. Generally, however, the forgivable flaws are those that add to our character, not character flaws.

Authentic leaders can sometimes gain loyalty even though lacking other important leadership traits. We came across such a situation while working in upstate New York several years ago. The conference center was in a beautifully wooded setting. A full palette of colors blazed across the tree-lined hills rising above the Hudson River. We were meeting with a group of executives from a multibillion-dollar company, a leader in its industry. During an afternoon break, we were on the lawn, deep in conversation with one of the participants about his frustrations with his boss.

"What is your opinion of him?" we asked.

"Do you really want to hear this?" he queried, while looking over the top of his glasses.

"Of course," we replied.

"Okay," he said, "I'll tell you. I think the guy is obsessed with status, loves to micromanage, and doesn't give two cents about how I feel about the situation."

"Sounds tough," we continued, "so why do you work so hard for him?"

"Well, this may sound funny, but even though he is a son-of-a-bitch, he's brilliant. He's nearly always right, he's on top of things, and I'm learning a great deal from him. We don't like each other, really, but I always know where

I stand with the guy. Sometimes he's a jerk and often he doesn't seem to care, but he lets you know that up front. I guess I admire his genuineness. He is who he is, no hidden agenda or pretense. And if my performance matches expectations, I get the credit and the rewards. He's a tough, but fair, boss."

This leader has maturity's closed fist but not its open hand, and still must learn to respect and serve others. Yet even though his maturity is stunted, followers respond to his authenticity. Authentic jerks are preferable to phony glad-handers.

Stories like this tend to add up over the years into an observable pattern. In fact, for years we have been asking middle and frontline leaders about their former role models and those role models' communication abilities. The following quotes capture the spirit of what they said:

"The guy simply told us like it was, in plain English."

"I knew what she was saying was true, because I'd watched her live her words."

"She wasn't afraid to let you know where she stood, show her true self."

"Even when the company was lying, we trusted him to tell the truth."

These people are describing leaders who do not cover the truth or their flaws with wax. It is often the cover-up, not the foul-up that results in career crashes. Wax is an attempt to fill the gap between what is said and what is done, between values professed and values practiced. Wax is the lie, the cover-up, the pretense, and the duplicity.

The Dance of Deception

Standing on the shores of Lake Wobegon, Garrison Keillor once said, "Sometimes you have to look reality right in the eye, and deny it." This makes great comedy, but it is a deadly leadership philosophy. Many well-intentioned business leaders, in an attempt to hold things together and keep things moving, make a dreadful leadership mistake. Whether out of an unconscious fear or deliberate malice, they dance around the truth.

Sometimes the dance is a quick Texas two-step, sometimes a long, passionate tango. We dance to avoid conflict. We dance because we need to be liked. We dance because we want to manipulate others. We dance because we are, in some way, afraid of the truth and the emotions the truth may stimulate in others. It happens when leaders and followers trade difficult truths for comfortable falsehoods, dangerous issues for safer ones, or a messy reality for a tidy make-believe. Like the tango, this dance takes two. Unlike the tango, it can involve hundreds or even thousands of people.

The dance starts with collusion. Leaders and followers publicly pretend to believe something, while each privately believes something different. It might be over something like job security. "This merger will have only positive effects."

ROI of Lies

We remember a situation in which an associate had clearly crossed an ethical line. The associate lied about significant personal travel expensed to a client project. The lie was clever, with a detailed backup story of misunderstood communications. Because we believed in her basic honesty, we danced. While never admitting any wrongdoing, she acted contrite and apologized for the *misunderstanding*, not the *fraud*. We pretended to believe the cover story, although we each knew the truth, and knew that we all knew. This was a lie but we all pretended it was not. Even though this violated values that trace their roots back to the small towns in Idaho and Oklahoma where we grew up, still we danced. Even though we preach that "client money is spent like our own," still we danced.

We all agreed to the pretense because we calculated the cost, in terms of time and energy, to be too great to confront the more difficult reality. We shook hands and all parties left, relieved the meeting was over but feeling a little corrupted for lying. Because the unspoken agreement seemed useful, we erroneously assumed it was a good leadership course. It was not. An opportunity for a stronger, cleaner relationship evaporated because we danced. The company was a little corrupted, but it survived. Our relationship with the individual survived, but was weakened. Our leadership survived, but our voice lost some of its volume.

Never again.

A dangerous game of psychological roulette is played whenever people deceive. It seems, on the surface, that collusion's Band-Aid is more effective than truth's iodine and suture. Over time, this collusion festers, creating lasting problems. As Chris Argyris points out in *Flawed Advice and the Management Trap*, even if the deception has momentary positive consequences, darker forces are at work. Describing why many projects fail, he writes:

> In the name of maintaining a good working relationship, all
> parties bypassed the truth and then covered up their bypass.
> The inevitable result: inner contradictions remain and frustra-
> tion grows. Thus, gaps and inconsistencies are not just problems
> of logic or argument. They are a recipe, a tested recipe, for
> bickering, dysfunctional behavior, and lackluster performance.

Every time your team avoids the critical "real issue," you lose. Every time the discussion outside the meeting room—physical or virtual—is dramatically different from the discussion inside the room, you lose.

Many leaders are unable to believe in others simply because they do not believe in themselves. Deceiving ourselves and deluding others damages and damns business leaders.

Authenticity

Authenticity combined with passion is the leader's megaphone. It amplifies the message above the clamor of downsizing or acquisitions, the whining of Wall Street, and the screams of competitors. Without authenticity, the facts, emotions, and symbols a leader communicates are muted.

The journey to greater authenticity begins when you identify the difference between what you believe and the truths you have inherited from others. Authentic leaders are more focused, centered, integrated, self-directed, and purposeful. Their need for approval, acceptance, status, deference, and even money diminishes as authenticity increases. Authentic leaders are dedicated to work that matters.

Authenticity liberates and relaxes. It requires much less energy to maintain balance. A leader's vulnerability stimulates courage in others and grants constituents permission to be themselves and speak the truth. Barriers dissolve and communication flows.

Leaders can often be identified through their courage. An emerging leader we know worked at a design firm full of flamboyant talent. For the purpose of protecting all parties, we will call him Antonio. He was a talented designer, who was religiously and politically conservative. He didn't swear, drink, or engage in the usual off-color repartee.

If there was ever an authentic and colorful CEO, it was Antonio's boss. He drove a Harley, peppered his speech with profanity, and, flouting company policy, kept a six-pack of beer in a small refrigerator under his desk. He owned a collection of what many considered to be world-class-ugly cowboy boots. This CEO didn't pretend to care about HR policy or practice political correctness. When a question came to his mind, he asked it.

One day, the CEO invited Antonio into his office. "I've got a question for you," he said. "What are your views on homosexuality?"

The question didn't surprise Antonio. He knew the CEO regularly blindsided folks. Even so, he would have preferred not tangling with his opinionated boss on this subject. His mind raced to find the right answer. He wanted to tell the truth but didn't want to offend. After a brief pause, he answered.

"I don't believe in sex outside marriage, so I guess you could say I don't discriminate."

Proud he could tell the truth with diplomacy, Antonio smiled. The CEO wasn't finished. "But you don't believe in homosexual marriage, right?" he pressed.

Antonio felt like he was in a real pickle. Nevertheless, he answered honestly, "Um, no. I guess there are a lot of different ways to say it, but I believe same-sex unions are a sin."

The CEO nodded, looking distraught. The creative design firm he headed employed more than a handful of gay employees. Some lived with partners who received health insurance. He felt proud to have a progressive company.

"Well," the CEO continued, "then how are you able to get along and work with some on our staff?"

Antonio remained authentic. "Well," he stated matter-of-factly, "I don't believe in swearing, drinking, or dirty jokes, and I get along with you."

The moment of truth had arrived. Antonio waited for what seemed like an eternity for the CEO's response.

"Hmmm, you're right. I can respect that."

Both men left with greater regard for themselves and for each other. Leadership stock at the design firm increased in that moment.

Leap of Faith

Leadership is ultimately an act of faith in other people. If you do not believe in yourself, it becomes difficult to believe in others. Maturity and authenticity help us believe in ourselves and our ability to lead. Lacking belief in ourselves and others undermines all attempts at leadership development.

An Authentic Leader

As president of Arby's, Don Pierce was responsible for communicating the strategic direction for the food chain's three thousand restaurants at the annual franchisers' meeting. While working with the company in the time leading up to the meeting, a senior executive privately expressed some concerns over Don's speaking ability. "Don is a great leader and a great communicator, but his last speech, his last couple of speeches were, uh, well, . . . boring," the executive said. "Could you work with him?"

It was a stunning remark. Don Pierce is a great strategist, a charming human being, and one of the least boring people you'd ever meet. Because Boyd and Don trusted one another, Boyd delivered the news matter-of-factly. "Don, the word on the street is that your last speech was pretty boring."

Laughing, Don replied, "Oh, it's worse than that. I've been working on public speaking for ten years just to get this bad."

His candor opened the door for some fast communication analysis. Others had written his recent speeches, and when he read them aloud in a group setting, he came across as a monotone, corporate CEO. Someone less than authentic. This was a concern because many of the powerful franchisers were resisting his progressive plans for Arby's. Don needed more power in his communication to help convince them. So, with much discussion, it was decided that he would approach the annual meeting with a simple plan to speak with conviction from memory. There would be no script. Don would focus on what he cared about the most—his strategic vision—and avoid the temptation of addressing other issues. Most important, he would just be himself.

This was easy because Don already knew what he wanted to

Effective leadership skills and behaviors are based on a belief in others. If you do not believe in others, you must pretend you do. This pretense warps leading into manipulating.

Kets de Vries observes, "Those leaders who are able to combine action with reflection, who have sufficient self-knowledge to recognize the vicissitudes of power, and who will not be tempted away when the psychological sirens that accompany power are beckoning will in the end be the most powerful."

say. He trashed the well-written script and placed poster-sized photos on easels on both sides of the meeting room. They showcased Arby's history. Don strolled between the easels as he spoke from personal memory of Arby's past. Having provided the background of where the company had been, he then approached a covered table at center stage. Lifting the cover off, he unveiled twenty-one different bottles of beer. People began to laugh, wondering where he was going with this demonstration.

"Who is the Budweiser of the QSR industry?" he asked, holding the Budweiser bottle above his head.

"McDonald's," several in the audience shouted. Picking up a Coors bottle, he stared at it with a questioning look and asked, "Burger King?"

As he held a Michelob aloft, someone shouted, "Wendy's!"

And then, changing to a more serious tone, he motioned to the remaining eighteen bottles and asked, "And who are we?"

This authentic approach using simple symbols created a terrific buzz in the room. Everyone wanted to talk about which bottle best represented his or her opinion of what Arby's stood for. And talk they did. At times, quite vociferously.

Regaining their attention, Don spoke from his heart about his dream for the Arby's brand and how he believed they could reach it. He shared his dream of brand development and dual branding. While some of the long-term Arby's loyalists still struggled to come to grips with the message, his vision was clearly and powerfully communicated. At the end of his speech, the same senior executive who had called Don boring rushed up and exclaimed, "Man, why didn't we tape this? The whole company needs to see this!"

Climbing
the Ladder
of Abstraction

Chapter Nine

The leader who creates a line of

sight between vision and task can inspire greatness.

Have you ever driven suddenly into a fog bank? You immediately slow down, gripping the steering wheel more tightly. If others are traveling with you, you shush their conversation. You instinctively try your bright lights, even though it didn't work the last ten times. You turn the radio down so you can see better. You lean over the steering wheel in an attempt to see three inches farther into the fog. You scan for the road stripes; those short-range markers guide you slowly ahead. You frantically check the rearview mirror, worried about your own taillights. The longer you drive in the fog, the more fatigued you become. Your perception of time alters.

Unfortunately, it's very likely that on occasion you have also worked in the fog. In this atmosphere, your mind can only focus on wanting out of the fog. Workers move at slower rates, teamwork degrades, stress levels increase, disengagement sets in, and productivity drops. Constituents, feeling a loss of clarity and control, cry out for more communication. In response, time-crunched, multitasking leaders work overtime "communicating."

However, without an overarching strategic vision and direction, leaders can find themselves creating messages rather than meaning. Responding independently to the needs of customers, employees, shareholders, and partners, they create a diverging stream of memos, speeches, letters, e-mails, and annual reports. These disparate messages can decrease visibility even further. Focusing either on the fast-moving strategic foreground of quarterly reports or on the slower-moving background of brand vision won't help. Clearing the fog requires foresight. *Vision* is the search for meaning. *Strategy* is the search for advantage. We define *foresight* as the search for both.

"He who predicts the future, lies, even if he tells the truth" is an Arab proverb worth repeating. Foresight is more about creating the future than predicting it. Constituents expect leaders to know the destination, even though it is uncertain, and the route, even though it will change. The leader's job is to build a shared image of the future, foster commitment, and orchestrate alignment.

The ABCs of Work

For a moment, consider that there are three levels of work required in a complex, technical society. Level A is doing work. Planning and organizing work is level B. Level C work creates unifying abstract concepts like vision, values, and brand identity. Many leaders do the first part of level C work reasonably well. They create a powerful strategic vision or compelling brand identity, but struggle to communicate it in a way that aligns customers, employees, partners, and shareholders. The inability to enlist others and maintain enrollment is a chronic leadership failure.

Changes in human nature occur more slowly than corporate culture yet more swiftly than drifting continents. Foresight is about understanding the relationship of fast and slow things, not merely focusing on rapidly changing things, like technology. Yes, Silicon Valley/Desert/Forest triangle, we are talking to you. Strategy and tactics, which are routes to the destination, are fast things. Destinations, like vision and identity, are slow things. Understanding the complex relationship of slow things to fast things gives a leader a deeper, broader perspective. It is level C work.

Stewart Brand, a founding member and director of Global Business Network, describes the dynamics of ecosystems and institutions, "Fast learns, slow remembers. Fast proposes, slow disposes. Fast is discontinuous, slow is continuous. Fast and small instructs slow and big by accrued innovation and occasional revolution. Fast gets all our attention, and slow has all the power. All durable dynamic systems have this sort of structure, it is what makes them adaptable and robust." Too much attention on technological fashion and too little attention on meaning and human nature create a leader who speaks in shallow sound bites and wins only fifteen minutes of fame. Adaptable? Yes. Robust? No.

Level of Abstraction

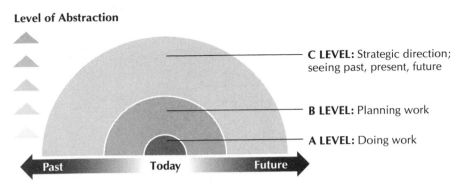

C LEVEL: Strategic direction; seeing past, present, future

B LEVEL: Planning work

A LEVEL: Doing work

Past Today Future

How Some Slow Things Got Faster

"The more information we amass, the more essential meaning becomes," says William Van Dusen Wishard, historian, futurist, and founder of World Trends Research. Human beings tend to act on information, learn from trial and error, and share what they have learned. If you accept these three tendencies as the underlying principles that drive the complexity of our time, a powerful cycle emerges. Information creates action, which creates learning. What's learned is shared, which creates more information, creating subsequent action. Which creates . . .

In ancient times, work was performed on an almost stationary stage. Visionary inventor Ray Kurzweil explains the rate of change in terms of paradigm shifts. During the agricultural age, paradigm shifts occurred over thousands of years. The industrial age produced paradigm shifts, first in a century and then in a generation. At the start of the information age, paradigms appeared to shift at the rate of three per lifetime. Kurzweil suggests that beginning in the year 2000, paradigm shifts have begun to occur at the rate of seven to ten per lifetime. Technology now advances at a rate that creates mind-numbing complexity, with confusion as its natural by-product. Kurzweil argues that "a merger between humans and computers that is so rapid and profound it represents a rupture in the fabric of human history" will produce what he terms a "singularity." He believes this event will take place sometime prior to the death of the last baby boomer. Just like the singularity of a black hole, natural laws and our ability to predict the future collapse. As the singularity approaches, trend analysis folds in on itself, crushing the ability to plan or predict. New technologies emerge before earlier ones are implemented, causing frustrating and discontinuous change. The importance of having a compelling level C construct and the difficulty of creating such a construct increase exponentially. Level C work is needed more than ever.

To succeed, the visionary must understand the nature of human beings and the meaning of work across time.

Climb the Ladder of Abstraction

"To solve any complex problem, we should first elevate our minds and view the situation from a higher dimension," encourages Kazuo Inamori, Chairman Emeritus of Kyocera Corporation. Traditionally, great companies have refined their business model within a paradigm and succeeded until the paradigm changed. Few have the ability to shift paradigm tracks, like how CSX successfully redefined its business from "railroad" to "transportation." As paradigms change more rapidly, they move from the category of slow things to fast things.

But as paradigms change at the rate of fashion, shifting alone is not enough. Business leaders also must select among paradigms in order to remain relevant. Elevation helps a leader see the past, present, and future as

The Foresight Process

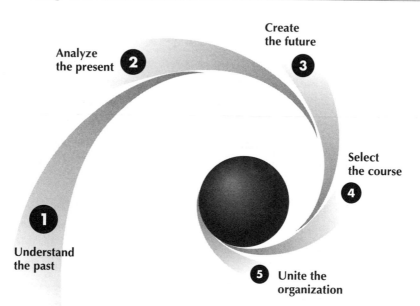

Analyze the present **2**

Create the future **3**

Select the course **4**

1 Understand the past

5 Unite the organization

a stream of history. Against the backdrop of time, fast-moving paradigms come into focus.

Scaling the Ladder of Abstraction prepares you for the Foresight Process. Research, trial and error, and pragmatism have helped us create a simple process for developing strategic vision, brand identity, or other level C models. The simultaneous development of a communication plan aids their adoption. The process seems to work in businesses of all sizes. It can be kept extremely simple or become as complex as the organization, industry, and situation require. It can be done in a few hours or expand into several months.

Understanding these concepts is crucial, because many leaders climb a few rungs to level B, discover a great strategy, and think their work is done. While strategies may indeed be found at level B, meaning comes from higher-order abstractions such as vision and brand identities. They can only be found at the top of the ladder—level C. Because foresight requires both strategy and vision, we must climb the Ladder of Abstraction. The Foresight Process helps us understand how to make that climb.

The Foresight Process

The Foresight Process has two fog-clearing objectives. First, leaders create a strategic direction, most often expressed as vision or brand identity. Second, they communicate a strategy to meet that vision in a way that unites and inspires.

Understand the Past

"Without understanding who we have been and what it has meant, it is difficult to reconceive where we are going or ought to go," writes Kathleen Hall Jamieson. Successful leaders link the symbolic past to the uncertain future. One way to do this is to begin by answering the question "What is our claim to greatness?" Understanding our historical greatness gives us confidence. Time lines, narratives, graphics, pictograms, multimedia, dioramas, and storytelling are used to create a historical record. Purpose, inspiration, and meaning are communicated through these records. From these symbolic records, select the key elements that must travel forward in time. Strategies, achievements, and the ability to cope with change are also conveyed. Consider the symbolic past with an eye toward the story it tells.

Analyze the Present

Examining trends, assessing competitive and technological threats, benchmarking best practices, evaluating a balanced scorecard, and taking the pulse of the organization's vital signs are techniques for analyzing the present. While analyzing the present, leaders are enticed to find an exciting new strategy. Because this new strategy answers so many pressing questions, it appears to be a vision, but is not. This results in "pseudovision" or brand strategy that changes rapidly and frustrates the organization.

Before moving on, make a list of those issues, ideas, and thought processes that may be important to share with your varied constituents. Next, consider how the story of the symbolic past is reflected in the present. Think of ways to use facts, emotions, and symbols to communicate these issues.

Create the Future

Understanding the past leans toward the symbolic. Analyzing the present leans toward the factual. Creating the future leans toward the emotional. Ultimately, you have to decide what you care about and aspire to accomplish. In business, there is generally the extraordinary goal vision, the great organization vision, or the combination of these two.

There are many creative processes that help leaders envision these worthy futures. The most important rule to follow during this phase is simple to articulate but difficult to practice: "Conceptsmith" first, and wordsmith second.

Conceptsmithing means polishing the ideas before polishing the language. Develop the key vision elements before crafting the vision statement. Using the information from the past and present, begin creating possible future scenes. Using a variety of creative processes, describe images of the desired future at the highest level of abstraction. Imagine the past, present, and future as a stream of history, keeping all in focus. Place yourself and your constituents in the evolving story.

Next, create your vision statement, making sure the words provide direction, unity, and inspiration. Most vision and mission statements are a series of bland, overused phrases like "leading the industry," being "employer of choice," or being "good corporate citizens." Superior vision statements tend to state a singular, powerful intent, such as LensCrafters' "helping the world to see." Let mission and value statements communicate additional meaning.

Select the Course

"Leaders conceive and articulate goals that lift people out of their petty pre-occupations, carry them above the conflicts that tear a society apart and unite them in pursuit of objectives worthy of their best efforts," wrote John W. Gardner. Selecting the course starts the trip back down the ladder and is a more pragmatic process involving the selection of core strategies or organizational imperatives. This requires courageous decision making. Because deciding upon strategic direction is important and takes time, leaders often rush toward implementation communication, in other words, orders. This precipitates the four fatal assumptions. Instead of using all their hard-earned communication work to unite and inspire, they descend the ladder too rapidly and return to communicating plans and projects.

Unite the Organization

We've heard it said that the difference between a vision and a hallucination is the number of people who see it. A leader's job is to unite his or her associates by helping them all see the same thing. This is the responsibility of leaders, not marketing or the communications department. We need to create a communication plan for the organization, and each leader needs to plan to communicate.

Using techniques borrowed from processes such as brand development, storyboarding, metaphor development, and screenwriting, a leader must consider the facts, emotions, and symbols of the story. It is like making a movie of the company's history and destiny that helps constituents see themselves as the action stars. By creating a rich plot, leaders can include customers, employees, shareholders, and partners in the same movie.

> By creating a rich plot, leaders can include customers, employees, shareholders, and partners in the same movie.

Sidney Lumet, a famous Hollywood director, has always maintained that the best movies are made when everyone is working to make the *same movie*. He recounts a memorable moment from his experience of shooting *The Sea Gull* in Sweden. The crew was deep in the woods, lighting a night scene. "An hour after nightfall, I drove out to the set. The road led over a hill. As the car came over the crest, I saw below me a small, concentrated, white-hot diamond. Everything around it was black except for this beautiful burst of light, where the set was being lit. It's a sight I'll always remember: people working so hard, all making the same movie, creating, literally, a picture in the middle of a forest in the middle of the night."

We encourage you to examine IBM's 2000 annual report for an example of effective metaphor use. This report reads like a novel. Here's how it starts:

You're ONE PAGE Away
from the NO-HOLDS-BARRED Story
of ONE year
in THE LIFE OF A COMPANY.

It's the story of
BIG BATTLES,
STINGING DEFEATS
&
GRITTY COMEBACKS.
UNEXPECTED ALLIANCES,
DARING FORAYS
&
GAME-CHANGING
DISCOVERIES.

In many ways
IT'S A STORY ABOUT THE FUTURE,
AS WELL AS THE RECENT PAST,
AND ABOUT ALL BUSINESS TODAY.
WHICH MEANS IT'S ABOUT E-BUSINESS.
AND ONE IN PARTICULAR.

Just remember that in every phase of the Foresight Process, diverge before you converge, and conceptsmith before you wordsmith.

Foresight Impairment

Most failed visions or failed brands do not die spectacular deaths; they simply collect digital dust on the company's Internet site. They are slowly forgotten, lost amid a whirlwind of work, changing priorities, and customer demands. Slogans are recycled rather than reinforced. Soon they are ignored, and sometimes mocked.

A Vision Statement Is Not a Vision

A vision statement is not the vision, an advertisement is not the brand, and a map is not the territory. The search for a compelling vision statement or the perfect ad campaign, while important, is not the first step. The goal is not to laminate the vision or billboard the ad, but to provide direction and to unite and inspire others. Vision and brands live in the hearts and minds of human beings, not in laminated wallet cards, posters, Web sites, or paperweights.

The worst-case lamination scenario is a senior team who has returned from an obligatory, annual off-site meeting with a well-crafted vision statement and a poorly crafted vision. Unfortunately, they didn't realize the danger of wordsmithing before conceptsmithing, so they have agreed upon the perfect words without agreeing upon the core ideas the words represent. Thus, each executive returns to his business unit extolling the same slogan but communicating a different vision.

On the other hand, a best-case scenario is to first align core vision concepts and then craft a powerful vision statement. United in concept, each leader can then elaborate on the vision statement in his or her unique, authentic voice.

Psuedoconsensus

Lee Burns, a Motorola middle manager, once observed during an off-site leadership conference, "It occurs to me that we have shared our visions, but we do not have a shared vision." We have worked with dozens, perhaps hundreds, of senior executive teams over the last fifteen years. Pseudoconsensus is their primary problem. Vision and strategies fall apart when members erroneously believe they agree or pretend they agree when they do not. This crumbling platform shakes as the executives leave the meeting. Each senior team member reinterprets the strategy and conveys messages to support his or her individual agenda. The independence, confidence, or even arrogance that helped them get to the "top" now prevents them from unifying around a common vision. Hearing different stories from different leaders, constituents smell the conflict. Court intrigue, while fascinating, leads to cynicism, anger, and revolt.

Unite and Inspire

The purpose of strategic vision and brand identity is to provide direction, unite, and inspire. It is difficult and rare to accomplish all three. Some people will allow themselves to be inspired only for brief periods, and others will never be inspired by your vision or brand. We recommend hiring people who are looking for a cause, not just a job, or people already inspired by your cause. Uniting inspired people is far easier than inspiring and uniting uninspired people.

Enrolling Others

Vision is a love affair with an idea. Like love, it needs to be communicated in small and big ways. Vision messages in a distributed network require simplicity, frequency, and alignment. Lacking these three characteristics, vision communication won't have the power to be heard above the network's natural static. The message must be simple if it is to flow easily through the network. Repetition fosters remembrance, so leaders should speak often. Raising hopes that a vision is imminent then poorly communicating the vision only increases the noise.

Mixed Messages

Alignment fails when the messages become mixed. Responding to the varied needs of customers, employees, shareholders, and partners, leaders can easily create four communication plans and strategies with four distinct sets of messages. Distributed networks share information, and each constituent group has immediate access to all communication streams. Disparate messages that contradict or invalidate one another increase uncertainty among all four groups.

Worldwide, businesses invest billions in brand development and brand advertising assisted by some incredibly creative talent. It must be disappointing when your employees watch these ads and say, "I'd like to work for a company like that."

How can you hope to have a dynamic brand without inspiring your associates? "The goal of an internal branding campaign is very similar to that of an external campaign: to create an emotional connection to your company,"

> **The creation of one set of messages that permeates our communication with all constituents is absolutely essential.**

writes Colin Mitchell, a senior partner at Ogilvy & Mather. A recent tompeterscompany! survey asked employees from over two hundred companies to respond to the question "Do you feel connected to your company's brand?" Fifty-one percent indicated they did not.

Analysts leave the quarterly conference call and then read information in a digital employee chat room that contradicts what they just heard. The "brand inside" message taints the "brand outside" message. Shareholders then listen to the analysts' doubts concerning management competence, which carries more weight than the torturous annual letter to the shareholders. The creation of one set of messages that permeates our communication with all constituents is absolutely essential. Mixed messages create fog. While you do not have control over how different constituents repeat your messages, you do have control over providing all of them with the same initial message.

FOG 101

There are many types of fog. We considered writing about radiation fog, evaporation fog, upslope fog, and advection fog. But all metaphors break down at some point. At the risk of going one image too far, however, we do suggest you consider one noxious form of fog, the dreaded inversion.

This weather phenomenon actually inverts temperature. In higher altitudes the air gets warmer, not colder. The first days of an inversion are foggy but manageable. In the same way, mixed messages cause some confusion, but management hopes things will clear over time. Executives who are talking about different visions add more hot air. Unfortunately, strong inversions don't allow the air to mix upward.

As a result, the longer the inversion lasts, the more pollution gets stuck in the fog. Fog gets dirty the longer senior management communication remains weak, infrequent, or lackluster, and tactics eclipse any sense of meaning. After a time, the fog has become smog. Workplace smog pollutes, driving talent to clearer climes. It is the surest sign informing us that all four fatal assumptions are in full operation and the leadership of the company has probably resorted to command-and-control communication.

Vision and Brands, Block by Block

In some instances, the Foresight Process evolves over time. For example, the LEGO Group's vision began as a specific and straightforward statement: "to become the world's strongest family brand by 2005." The executive team was inspired and passionate, but employees responded with, "OK. So what?" LEGO executives realized that *choosing* a vision is just a beginning.

The word LEGO is derived from the two Danish words *Leg Godt,* meaning "play well." LEGO executives added the concept of "lifelong creativity" to the vision. The new vision involved "nurturing the child in each of us" and stimulating learning "through creativity and imagination." LEGO executives truly believed that if they preached lifelong creativity to customers, they could also practice it internally. They wanted to create a "truly global organization where employees are open-minded, crave new impulses and are prepared to challenge traditional ways of working and learning." This idea was deeply rooted in LEGO brand history, and the vision began to develop meaning in the hearts and minds of the employees.

The company embarked on an ambitious, long-term strategy to implement its vision. In 1996, the company opened LEGOLAND Windsor in the United Kingdom, the first LEGO theme park to open outside the original 1968 Denmark LEGOLAND. Parks followed in California and Germany. In 1998, LEGO launched Mindstorms, expensive and creative robotic toys developed through a partnership with MIT. In 1999, the company signed a revolutionary licensing deal with George Lucas and created a Star Wars line of LEGO products. It continued this idea with Winnie the Pooh and Harry Potter deals. These product launches have been wildly successful for customers and the company.

Recently, LEGO has developed Serious Play, a business unit that uses LEGO technology to stimulate level C thinking with business teams. "Here's a LEGO elephant, a racecar, and a house with no windows," says Robert Rasmussen, COO and creative director of Serious Play, to a group of executives. "Which one of these is like your company?" Two-day on-site workshops, led by select consultants, use the unusual to stimulate higher-order thinking.

LEGO's vision and strategy has increased sales and taken revenues above the $1 billion mark for the first time in the company's history. Despite media criticism over sluggish profits, the company promises to stick to its vision. Lifelong creativity involves "challenging traditional ways." Becoming the world's "strongest" family brand involves much more than just selling plastic bricks as the company did for its first sixty years.

Line of Sight

Translating brands and visions into tasks is a difficult challenge. The leader who creates a line of sight between vision and task can inspire greatness. Here is what Ronald H. Henderson Jr., captain of the USS *John F. Kennedy*, said shortly before the *JFK*, sailing in the north Arabian sea, launched her first strikes into Afghanistan for Operation Enduring Freedom.

> Good evening on board John F Kennedy, Carrier Air Wing SEVEN, and Carrier Group Six.
>
> We are currently proceeding, at best speed, to our launch point for tonight's strikes, off the coast of Pakistan, nearly 700 miles south of our targets in Afghanistan.
>
> At midnight, CVW 7 will launch into the dark night, and strike their first blows of Operation Enduring Freedom, the war on terrorism. For us this is a culminating point in space, a culminating point in time, and a culminating point in history.
>
> Our enemy is a group of religious fanatics, who pervert the peace of Islam and twist its meaning to justify the murder of thousands of innocents at the Twin Towers of New York, at the Pentagon, and in a field in Pennsylvania. They hate us and attack us because they oppose all that is good about America. They hate us because we are prosperous. They hate us because we are tolerant. They hate us because we are happy. Mostly, they hate us because we are free and because we will "pay any price, bear any burden, meet any hardship, support any friend or oppose any foe to assure the survival and success of liberty." Make no mistake—this is a fight for Western Civilization. If these monsters are not destroyed they will destroy us, and our children and children's children will live in fear forever.
>
> America is the only nation that can stop them and destroy them. Only America has the strength of character and the vast

resources to hunt these fanatics down anywhere in the world. We have friends and Allies but we are the leaders of the world our forefathers made and died for. Our Naval power has been the principal weapon of our resolve. Great ships and great crews have gone before us—ENTERPRISE, CARL VINSON, KITTY HAWK, TEDDY ROOSEVELT, JOHN STENNIS. Tonight, our enemies will feel the power of USS JOHN F KENNEDY. It is now our turn to strike for justice and we will strike hard.

Millions of Americans wish they could be here with us tonight. They saw the Twin Towers fall, and watched helplessly, wanting to do something to defend America and our way of life. For us tonight, that wait and that helplessness are over. We have reached the point where we are all part of something so much greater than ourselves. For the rest of our lives, no matter whether we stay in the Navy or move on to civilian life, no matter what we do or where we go, we will remember that on 10 March 2002, we came together and struck a blow for freedom.

All of us are volunteers. Most of us joined the Navy to serve our country and better ourselves. Tonight, and in the nights to come, we are given the opportunity of a lifetime, a chance to truly make a difference in the world. Our namesake John F. Kennedy wrote that "a single person can make a difference, and every person should try." Tonight, WE make a difference! We represent America in all its power and diversity. We are men and women, rich and poor, black and white, and all colors of the human rainbow. We are Christian, Jew, and yes, Muslim. WE ARE AMERICA.

This war will not be short, pleasant, or easy. It has already required the sacrifice of our firefighters, our policemen, our soldiers, our Sailors, our airmen, and our Marines. More sacrifices will be made. In the end we will win, precisely because we are those things that the terrorists hate—prosperous, happy, tolerant, and most of all, free.

Those Americans who wish they could be here with us are, in fact, here with us in spirit. Never before in American history has our nation been so completely unified and resolute in purpose.

Every one of them is cheering us on, praying for our safety and our success. Our families are behind us 100%. We will not let them down. We are, and will be, men and women of honor, courage, and commitment.

I believe, as Abraham Lincoln said, that, "America is the last, best hope for the world." Tonight we hold a shining beacon of that hope. We shall keep it burning brightly.

Stay sharp. Stay focused. Stay safe. Use the training that has made you the best Sailors in the world, the best Sailors in the history of the world. Trust in your faith, and in your shipmates. God bless us all, and God bless America.

We asked Captain Henderson what he hoped to accomplish with the message. He said, "[These] are young, uncomplicated men and women, who overcome great hardships to accomplish anything we ask of them. . . . I wanted them to understand the importance of their tasks, even the seemingly trivial ones, and stay focused on those tasks at hand." We also asked about the impact of his message. "I believe that I was successful in motivating and focusing the crew. . . . It inspired them to think of themselves as part of an elite, special team. . . . Many crewmembers have spoken to me about the message, and thanked me for it—a fact I find ironic, because my intent was to honor and thank *them*."

Lift the fog. Unite and inspire. Honor their contributions.

OneVoice

Leaders must communicate a million complicated things when they fail to communicate a few, simple, profound ones.

As the helicopter maneuvered through the fog, enshrouding Monte Marmolada in the Southern Alps near Agordo, Italy, Dave Browne's guts churned. He wasn't as much concerned about the flight as he was about what was waiting for him on the ground. He was meeting with Leonardo Del Vecchio, the Sam Walton of Italy, whose successful hostile takeover of LensCrafters' parent company, U.S. Shoe, made him Dave's new boss. Del Vecchio's Luxottica, formerly a vendor, was now the parent company. Dave was considering what he was going to say to his ten thousand associates upon his return to the United States. Two metaphors came to his mind. "We've climbed one mountain and now have another one to climb." Looking at the fog blanketing the valley below him, he thought, "If we hold hands, stick together and keep moving, we can make it to the top of an even higher mountain."

Dave and Leonardo's first meetings were extremely professional and polite. Leonardo was gracious and patient with his newest acquisition. However, they spoke different languages, both literally and metaphorically. Luxottica was a brand-driven company; LensCrafters, a vision- and values-driven company. Luxottica was a wholesaler and manufacturer; LensCrafters, a retailer.

Dave was determined that LensCrafters would not lose "the heart that made the company special," while Luxottica would get an exceptional return on their investment. As he talked with his associates, he communicated the symbolism of climbing mountains and navigating fog. "The metaphor helped us get through a year of uncertainty," he said. He told associates that if they needed help, all they had to do was "hold each other's hands a little tighter."

Speaking about his relationship with Leonardo, Dave said, "The language and cultural differences were challenging, but, surprisingly, we first really connected at a heart level." Claudio Del Vecchio, Leonardo's son and an exceptional executive in his own right, embraced "the Gift of Sight" program and then helped his father to visualize it. These three senior leaders all felt strongly about the company's vision of "helping the world to see," and the Gift of Sight program, "giving the gift of sight to those who have the least and need us the most." The common ground helped clear the business fog as acquirer and acquired began to see the same future. Dave describes the experience from that point on as "the smoothest hostile takeover in history."

LensCrafters has been blessed with three excellent CEOs. Ban Hudson fueled early growth and engineered the vision and values that inspired exceptional performance. Dave Browne found that not only did his head add value to business, but his heart did as well. Current CEO Cliff Bartow's retail acumen and clarity has led the company to new heights of growth and profits. Each helped the organization to accomplish more; each added his unique voice to the core themes of the organization. These are leaders of integrity, character, and commitment. They used their passion for ideals and persistent hard work to create what we call a OneVoice company.

Whenever we find a OneVoice company like LensCrafters or TNT, we find paradoxical magic. First a higher-order, symbolic message emotionally unifies all constituents. Second, relentless execution translates the meaningful ideal into meaningful work. As the late Ezra Taft Benson, former Secretary of Agriculture and president of the Church of Jesus Christ of Latter Day Saints once said, "Vision without work is dreamery. Work without vision is drudgery. Vision with work is destiny."

A senior Harley-Davidson executive explained, "What we sell is the ability for a forty-three-year-old accountant to dress in black leather, drive through small towns and have people be afraid of him." The highly celebrated Harley-Davidson is a OneVoice company. Check out the alignment. Visit their Web site, read their annual report, and drive into one of their dealerships.

Metaphor Studio in Cincinnati is a small OneVoice company. This talented group of creative artists and dedicated programmers talk about one thing only—great customer experience. Each and every meeting begins with the question, "What's the customer experience going to be?"

Jayne-Anne Gadhia was a banker in pursuit of a dream. Just as Richard Branson's Virgin had transformed the traditional businesses of planes and trains, she wanted to transform finance. In 1994 Jayne-Anne put action to imagination as she helped set up and lead Virgin Direct, a jargon-free, consumer-focused financial services company. In 1997, she leveraged the success of Virgin Direct into the revolutionary Virgin *One* account. The basic concept of Virgin *One* is to put all of a customer's money—meaning checking, savings, brokerage, mortgage, and everything else—into one account. The idea challenged the rules of banking. Jayne-Anne built this business against all the odds and expert opinion. "Everyone said it was going to fail," she told us. Her relentless communication of this single idea attracted daring associates. With the support of her boss, in under three years she and her eight hundred dedicated personnel built Virgin *One* into a company of seventy thousand customers and a mortgage book of £4 billion.

A Million Complicated Messages

Leaders must communicate a million complicated things when they fail to communicate a few simple profound ones. Consider the thousands of messages from your company to your four main constituencies—your shareholders, customers, employees, and partners. If you are typical, different groups inside your company have different message responsibilities. The CFO and investor relations own the shareholders' messages. Marketing owns the consumer brand messages. Human resources or the communications department owns internal messages. The chief operating officer owns strategy messages. Add sales, training, public relations, and whoever owns the company Web site, and you have the likelihood of a million mixed messages.

The OneVoice magic combines a high-level symbolic message with flawless execution, producing the best chance for unity and success.

Branding — The Next Thing

Every few years the business community grapples with complexity and derives a savior—a new concept, a new idea that will carve structure from chaos and point out the right direction. Branding seems to be the new, saving concept. It attempts to create OneVoice, one unifying element, one collection point for our disparate, confusing messages.

Broadly defined brands tell your customers what you promise, your associates what you stand for, your vendors what you need, and your investors what you'll do. Brand is the new battleground for distinction, attempting to gain attention and maintain interest.

Friction, Confusion, and Malperformance

According to Peter Drucker, "The only things that happen naturally in an organization are friction, confusion and malperformance. Everything else is the result of leadership." Inconsistent messages fuel all three destructive elements.

The responsibility for speaking in "one voice" rests squarely on the shoulders of an organization's senior leadership team. Peter Senge asserts, "Every organization has a destiny: a deep purpose that expresses the organization's reason for existence." The entire senior leadership team must communicate the same "destiny" and "deep purpose" in order to speak with OneVoice.

Alignment is primarily an emotional, not logical, process. Yet managers spend 90 percent of their time aligning facts and 10 percent on the more difficult task of aligning hearts and minds.

The Fire Within

Just past midnight on February 5, 2002, Bob Chambers stood waist-deep in snow, six thousand feet up the side of Twin Peaks Mountain. The wind chilled the temperature to zero. Bob held a seven-foot pole in one hand and a cell phone in the other. His L.L. Bean Two-Layer Duofold underwear kept his body warm, but passion warmed his heart. He was part of a grand movement called the Olympics. Working toward this moment, he hadn't thought about the scandal or bribery that had plagued the beginning of the Salt Lake Games. He hadn't thought that much about the money his company would make. "This," he told us, "was the highlight of my career."

From the steps of Utah's capitol building, 1952 gold medalist and Utah resident Stein Erickson pointed the Olympic torch toward Twin Peaks and Bob flipped the switch. In an instant, the compact fluorescent lightbulbs sitting atop 1,850 poles illuminated five giant interlocking rings stretching more than three football fields across the mountain. At the same time, fireworks exploded and the crowd cheered. Over the next seventeen days, more than three billion people would see the "floating rings," which were large enough to be seen from outer space.

Scott Givens served as managing director for the creative group of the

Salt Lake Organizing Committee (SLOC). He had been charged with integrating the theme "Light the Fire Within," first developed by creative ad man Gordon Bowen. In March 2000, the organizing committee's president, Mitt Romney, endorsed the theme and it was announced to the world. It could have been just another inspirational theme, but these leaders were committed to aligning the hearts and minds of their employees, hundreds of vendors, and approximately thirty thousand volunteers. As Mitt Romney said when we talked with him, "We were able to align the interest of the various parties because we all share, as a human family, some pretty common values."

The SLOC realized that they had the chance to write a chapter in the one-hundred-year-old Olympic book. They started with the Coca-Cola-sponsored torch relay, selecting 11,500 runners from over 100,000 inspiring stories of people who wanted to carry the metal and glass torch, lighted by a flame inside.

"Mitt and I had long conversations about having everything aligned," Scott said. "We could get an *A* in the opening ceremonies, an *A* in the medal presentations, and an *A* at the venues, but we needed all the *A*s to be aligned in order to become valedictorians."

Scott defined the design criteria that helped the creative group. "I actually wrote a five-page outline of who we are and who we aren't," he said. "I wrote hard and fast rules." He said the intensity of the theme and the definition provided by the rules liberated the sponsors, vendors, and volunteers to add their own voice to one inspiring idea. "The walls allowed us to be more creative, because we knew who we were. It let the artists and the writers really look at ways to stretch themselves within the walls."

Scott says the ever-present "Children of Light" was an idea that came directly from a vendor responsible for the opening ceremony. The children were added to all events and ceremonies. Carrying a small lantern, they escorted every medal winner to the stand. "All our staff was looking for ways to bring the theme in." The colors of the banners and signs communicated the theme. People walking through downtown Salt Lake could see the colors heat from cool blues to hot oranges as they approached the medals plaza. The theme was etched into each and every Olympic medal awarded, something the International Olympic Committee had never before allowed. Actions and details like these helped the entire Olympic organization align behind the inspiring concept of "Light the Fire Within."

Olympic Communication Principles

In our conversation with Scott Givens, three principles emerged. First, a simple, deeply symbolic theme can align the hearts and minds of thousands. "It was the simplicity that was so great," Scott said. "People owned and interpreted and used it in their own ways."

Second was the importance of discipline. "Mitt was a great partner, because he always checked me," Scott said. "If we were not aligned, he immediately saw it."

The third principle was how a disciplined leadership used a powerful theme to naturally align disparate constituencies. "Alignment was not forced," Scott said. In an organization with thousands of employees, thousands of volunteers, hundreds of vendors, and billion-dollar budgets, it's impossible to force alignment. Scott Givens couldn't be everywhere, write every script, and design every sign. "The best part of alignment is people getting in line on their own."

Bob Chambers's company, It's Alive Co., was just one vendor; yet, he knew exactly what to do. "It was pretty easy to tell as we were going through the process that the organizing committee didn't make a distinction between our project and other projects," he said. "It was all about turning the entire city into a vision of light."

Walking through the SLOC's offices in Salt Lake City a few weeks after the games, associates talked about the "flicker" that was still within them. The fire had sustained them during the seventeen days of the games as they "fought the tired within." Even those few employees who finished up the work quipped, "We'll leave the light on for you."

Olympic Business

For companies like Coca-Cola, and other sponsors, the Olympics are huge business. Haven Riviere was responsible for Coca-Cola's multimillion-dollar sponsorship. "They were consistent in their theme all the way through," he said. "That was extremely important to us. If they had changed, people would not have seen the connection between what they were doing and what we were doing. The powerful thing that Salt Lake did was to recognize that they had multiple groups. That they had to work with athletes, the viewers, the fans in the stand, and the marketing sponsors."

Mitt Romney and the leadership of the SLOC spoke with OneVoice. "The common vision of what we were hoping to accomplish was something that everyone could buy into," Romney told us. "Our vendors and sponsors saw something that communicated their values." Salt Lake wasn't about scandal, bribery, or commercialism. It wasn't even about September 11. Without a strong symbolic theme, it could have been about any of those things.

Winter games never outperform summer games, yet Salt Lake brought in more sponsorship dollars than Atlanta. Here are the numbers:

- Salt Lake sold $173 million in tickets, twice the number sold at Nagano in 1998.
- A record $545 million in broadcast rights attracted 2.5 times the normal prime-time audience.
- 250,000 visitors came to Utah, spending $350 million.
- Salt Lake City ended up with a net gain of nearly $3.6 million from the 2002 Winter Games.
- Salt Lake City realized a total economic impact of $4.8 billion.
- Salt Lake experienced 149 percent over prime-time averages. In 1994, Lillehammer experienced just 130 percent.
- The Salt Lake games repaid the state $59 million in diverted sales tax revenue and has promised millions more in "legacy" funds to help operate venues for decades to come.

Fraser Bullock, Romney's right-hand man, told Salt Lake City's *Deseret News* about Mitt's work ethic. "I'm the one that saw what Mitt did day in and day out, getting on planes, working seven days a week, and I knew how dire the financial situation was. What Mitt did was absolutely turn around the Games, and there's no question in my mind. . . . I think without Mitt's leadership the Games would have happened, but they may have left a taxpayer bill, they would not have run nearly as well as they did and I don't think we would have shown as well to the world as we did. His leadership is all over the success of the Games." In *The New York Times,* Lloyd Ward, the chief executive of the United States Olympic Committee said, "Salt Lake was almost a rebirth of the Olympic mark and our brand equity." Bob Chambers put it this way: "The better job that we do in getting all the individual pieces to align with the larger idea, the more it shows through to the audience watching it."

Years from now people will remember the "Children of Light." They'll remember the giant Olympic Rings on Twin Peaks. Fifty years from now when Jimmy Shea's granddaughter competes in the skeleton at the Sun Valley Olympic games, she'll brandish the gold her grandfather won in Salt Lake. Etched into the medal for the entire world to see will be the words: "Light the Fire Within."

LAST WORD

Calling All Capitalists

L eaders act in a stream of history," wrote John W. Gardner. On September 10, 2001, Rudolph Giuliani was a lame-duck mayor struggling with cancer and mired in a divorce scandal. One hundred and twelve days later he was named *Time* magazine's "Person of the Year." Context shifted and Rudy responded with competence and caring.

Understanding the significance of the moment is important, but great communicators understand the larger reality that surrounds every situation. As we evaluated the best communicators, we observed that they were not as tempted by the trivial. Because they viewed each day against a larger back-drop, they were able to select the most important facts, emotions, and symbols to communicate. They seemed to effortlessly connect the timely with the timeless. Leaders get context right when they see themselves and their con-stituents as actors across time, rather than as puppets on a momentary stage.

The Birth of a Revolution

To gain greater appreciation for the powerful technical and social forces that are altering our work lives, let's click to The History Channel. In 1445 few appreciated the flood of both intellectual exploration and economic prosper-ity Johannes Gutenberg's press would unleash. The world's library expanded from thirty-five thousand to perhaps as many as ten million books in less than fifty years. Over the span of two generations, the world changed from one where information was held by the rich and powerful to one where infor-mation was available and readable by the most common of families. As many as ten thousand monks who had held esteemed positions as calligraphers and copiers of texts, employed by a religious monopoly, were outsourced by moveable type. Printing companies created a new entrepreneurial class who rose from the ranks of nonaristocratic rabble. As the printer's hardware became more common, publishers gained dominance because of their increasing ability to control content. The proliferation of the moveable type press was a stimulus for the scientific and artistic Renaissance, religious Reformation, and political Revolutionary eras. If a printing press can change the nature of work and the world, imagine what modern technologies will do.

Inventing the New World of Work

For the foreseeable future, information will be the business resource, and innovation the work (read this sentence three times before proceeding). The organizational structure that best fits this future is the distributed network. Creating alignment in a distributed network is more difficult than in either a hierarchy or a matrix. Communication in a hierarchy goes up and down, and in a matrix it goes in, out, and across. In both cases, the communication generally travels along predetermined lines, propelled by power and procedure. A distributed network by design demands a free flow of resources and communication. Hierarchies and matrices share power as the fundamental organizing principle. A distributed network, however, is organized around the work itself. Everything is organized and reorganized to support one thing—work that matters. Communication in a distributed network is powered by message relevance and leader credibility. The Leader's Voice is heard above the natural, chaotic noise of the network.

The transition from hierarchies of the industrial age to modern matrix structures produced tremendous productivity increases. It used to take America's auto manufacturers seven years to go from concept to production model. Now, they can do it in less than twenty-four months. Distributed networks promise even greater productivity gains through new frontiers of organization structure and individual contribution.

"In an era when terrorists use satellite phones and encrypted email, U.S. gatekeepers stand armed against them with pencils and paperwork and archaic computer systems that don't talk to each other," reported *The Boston Globe* on September 30, 2001. Law enforcement and the military are altering structures to match the realities of war, just as businesses are altering structure in order to compete. In both cases, communication, more than power, creates passionate alignment.

The Meaning of Work

Our grandfathers were farmers. Farming by nature has meaning and purpose. If they did a good job during the summer, their families ate all winter. They seeded every spring and celebrated harvest every fall. Our fathers were men of the Industrial Age. They built things. At the end of their lives there were buildings and machines where none had been before.

Driving along State Highway 33 through Idaho's Snake River Valley, Boyd and his father, Ray, experienced a rare moment. Ray was a bricklayer. He had the thick calluses and Popeye forearms that are signatures of his trade. Ray was ill, and the unspoken reality between him and his son was the limited time Ray had left. As they passed through the valley, Ray pointed out the many buildings he had built. Boyd said, "Dad, many of these buildings will be here even long after I'm gone."

"Not a bad way to spend a life," Ray said.

Boyd saw the expression on his father's face as he completed this simple statement. It was the same look of satisfaction Boyd had observed as a youngster, as he had cleaned and packed his father's tools. Ray would arrive on a flat patch of land one day and then, not long after, would leave the job site, admiring the building that had not been there before.

We are consultants.

Nothing we do feels permanent. Our teaching, coaching, and consulting constantly evolve. Tangibility, permanence, beginnings, and endings are elusive. It is tough to know when to celebrate. There is no harvest marker that rallies us, or our colleagues, to celebration.

Individuals have always been defined, in part, by their work. The surname "Clarke" is derived from the work title "clerk." Today, many workers feel outmoded and struggle to stay relevant. Just at the moment "work" has attained the state of early philosophers' dreams, days spent working with ideas and people, it seems to have lost meaning.

But work has meaning, despite the general ennui that sometimes surrounds it. We look back over the course of our work with customers and it is easy to remember careers we have helped, situations we have turned around, and organizations we have impacted. There are few tangible clues to these accomplishments, but the results have been real. Recalling these stories adds more meaning to our work than counting our financial success.

Most American workers are "consultants," peddling ideas and organizing information. We all perform skilled service and information work based upon some contractual agreement. And we are willing to bet that many managers, if not most, have grappled with the serious issue of work's meaning. In our minds, leaders who create a meaningful work context have accomplished a difficult and significant task. When their work matters, constituents will volunteer extra hours, work harder, expend more energy, and naturally increase their contribution to esprit de corps. Give them a reason.

Innovation Is Everyone's Business

As the sparkle of new millennium fireworks fell from the Eiffel Tower, the world's business gurus gathered on hallowed ground for a level-four harmonic convergence. With stars and planets aligned, they inspected the corporate entrails of the previous century and agreed, one and all, that the *new* new thing, the new main thing, the new holy grail of corporate success in the new century would be innovation.

We agree!

Innovation is creativity in its working clothes. It has experimentation as a coworker and failure as a strategic partner. Alone, technology doesn't guarantee innovation. Only the practiced discipline of innovation will produce innovative results. Henry Petroski wrote in *To Engineer Is Human* that "no one wants to learn by mistakes, but we cannot learn enough from successes to go beyond the state of the art." While failure can be painful, innovative companies embrace this pain. If you want more innovation, allow more experiments.

The communication challenge for innovation is complex. Because businesses last only when financial successes outweigh failures, rapid prototyping and experimentation cannot be used as a license for anarchy. Leaders will have to communicate the limits of both boundary and process as they encourage innovation. Both freedom and boundaries are established by message clarity and thematic repetition.

The Golden Age of Talent

Talent retention is a euphemism that describes the individual and organizational struggle to adapt to a distributed network. Employment matters. People have to make money. Production matters. Companies have to make profits. Individuals and companies must learn to produce in a distributed network.

The individual, 401(k) and benefits in hand, now travels from company to company as a complete business unit. If a person's skills are not valuable or distinctive, he or she descends the economic ladder. As white-collar robots evolve and machines do more information work, employment opportunities will depend upon unique, human capabilities such as synthesis, creativity, compassion, and leadership.

To Brand Is Human

Today, good quality and good service are merely tickets into the marketplace, but neither confers advantage. "While everything may be better, everything is increasingly the same," declares Paul Goldberger.

Kjell Nördstrom and Jonas Ridderstråle pegged it in *Funky Business: Talent Makes Capital Dance:* "The 'surplus society' has a surplus of similar companies, employing similar people, with similar educational backgrounds, coming up with similar ideas, producing similar things, with similar prices and similar quality."

A brand is worth no more than the customer's last experience with a brand touch point. Distinction lies in leaders branding inside the company as vigorously as they brand outside the company. The communication problem for branding inside is intimidating. As skilled as leaders have become at communicating brand identity to customers, they are woefully inconsistent and uninspiring at communicating the message internally. In fact, the messages they communicate to customers, employees, and investors often feel unrelated. The formal messages sent via advertising, vision statements, analyst conference calls, annual reports, and Web sites usually lack alignment and sometimes conflict. We can't tell if these are mixed messages or mixed-up messages. Our advice to leaders: Stop saying everything and start saying something.

The Reorganization of Planet Earth

Recent polls indicate that half of all baby boomers imagine one hundred years to be a realistic lifespan. Those who have mapped the human genome may have enabled a two-hundred-year lifespan for the next generation. Dr. William Haseltine from Human Genome Sciences, in an interview with The Motley Fool, said:

> . . . our task is to couple individual immortality to the essential immortality of life itself, and I believe through stem cell replacement, we have a clear vision of how to achieve it. Whether we will do it in the next 100 years or beyond one cannot predict. But we now know the potential is there and we believe it can be achieved.

Democracy and freedom were academic ideas 250 years ago. Today, democracy governs more individuals than any other political system. In 1946 there were seventy-six countries in existence. Today there are more than two hundred. Democracy, freedom, and the rise of the knowledge worker have created opportunities as our focus shifts from things to ideas.

But a problem lurks. Some dreams take money. As economist Hernando de Soto writes concerning people in underdeveloped societies, "They have houses but not titles; crops but not deeds; businesses but not statutes of incorporation. It is the unavailability of these essential representations that explains why people who have adapted every other Western invention, from the paper clip to the nuclear reactor, have not been able to produce sufficient capital to make their domestic capitalism work." Democracy allows individuals to own and borrow against tangible assets, creating capital that is then used to purchase dreams and build companies.

Calling All Capitalists

Which new technologies will save us? None. It is not our technologies alone that have advanced us or held us back. Dysentery kills more children each day than any other disease, yet basic medical technology can cure it. We can communicate with anyone, anywhere with technology, yet the dialogue between even friendly nations is often strained and strident. We have the technology to feed everyone, yet millions die of hunger each year. Our most challenging problems are not now, nor have they ever been, technical. It is our social systems that fail us.

The basic principles we use to organize ourselves are the clear predictors of success for nations, businesses, communities, and teams. For years we have followed the literature concerning the economic success of nations. Three characteristics are at the top of most scholars' lists: extreme freedom, rule of law, and moderate climate. The top two are social principles. Apparently these two can even overcome the effects of immoderate climate.

We are passionate capitalists. Communism, while a noble philosophy, fails as a social system due to irreparable flaws. The difference between a prosperous Europe and the struggling Soviet Republics is even more dramatic when you consider the technological prowess of the former Soviet Union. Capitalism, like communism, has flaws. Capitalism, as an economic philosophy, can fail and in many ways has lost its way. Democracy with capitalism is a social system that grants the greatest opportunity to the greatest number and has the greatest chance for success. As de Soto explains

> With its victory over communism, capitalism's old agenda for economic progress is exhausted and requires a new set of commitments. It makes no sense continuing to call for open economies without facing the fact that the economic reforms underway open the doors only for small and globalized elites and leave out most of humanity. At present, capitalist globalization is concerned with interconnecting only the elites that live inside the bell jars. To lift the bell jars and do away with property apartheid will require going beyond the existing borders of both economics and law.

Like de Soto, we do not propose a socialized redistribution of wealth, but rather an expansion of economic opportunity provided by the combination of democracy and capitalism. Capitalism's new context must include commitments that unlock the social and technical power of the many, rather than being used solely as a mechanism for increasing the wealth of the few.

Just as social system failures are at the heart of the world's economic problems, they are at the heart of most business problems. Historically, leaders with passionate voices have driven positive social changes in countries and companies.

Boyd Clarke   Ronald Crossland

NOTES

FIRST WORD

xiii   *James Earl Jones:* James Earl Jones and Penelope Niven, *James Earl Jones: Voices and Silences* (New York: Touchstone Books, 1994), pp. 65-66.

CHAPTER 1. THE BIRTH OF A LEADER

4   *Golda Meir:* Michael Avallone, *A Woman Called Golda* (New York: Leisure Books, 1982), pp. 164-65.

6   *Gardner quote:* John W. Gardner, *On Leadership* (New York: The Free Press, 1990), p. 24.

10   *Dave Browne,* personal interview, April 8 and 9, 2002.

13   *Communication with horses:* Monty Roberts, *The Man Who Listens to Horses* (New York: Random House, 1997), and personal interview, March 6, 2002.

CHAPTER 2. HARDWIRED FOR FACTS, EMOTIONS, AND SYMBOLS

20   *Phineas Gage:* several sources, including <http://www-instruct.nmu.edu/psychology/mmacmil/gage_page/pgage.htm>.

21   *Damasio quote:* Antonio R. Damasio, *Descartes' Error: Emotion, Reason, and the Human Brain* (New York: Putnam, 1994), p. 52.

21   *Pinker quote:* Steven Pinker, *How the Mind Works* (New York: Norton, 1997), p. 370.

23   *2001 Employee engagement survey: Gallup Management Journal, 2001.*

23   *Additional data:* Marcus Buckingham and Curt Coffman, *First, Break All the Rules: What the World's Greatest Managers Do Differently* (New York: Simon & Schuster, 1999), p. 33.

24   *Supplee Group survey:* "Employees Cite Poor Managers as Primary Reason for Quitting," PR Newswire (Jan. 28, 2002), <http://www.ecruitinginc.com/news/news.asp?ID=360>.

24   *Lou Harris and Associates and Los Angeles Times-Mirror:* "Strategic Vision: A New Role for Corporate Leaders," Study No. 855018, conducted for Learning International, Inc., December 1985 to February 1986, p. 40.

24   *How effective are your senior executives:* Authors' research, 1988.

24   *Mirvis and Kanter:* Donald L. Kanter and Philip H. Mirvis, *The Cynical Americans: Living and Working in an Age of Discontent and Disillusion* (San Francisco: Jossey-Bass, 1989), p. 10.

28   *Demosthenes:* Edmund Fuller, editor, *Lives of the Noble Greeks* (New York: Dell, 1959), pp. 354-56.

Chapter 3. How TNT Found Drama

35ff   Jennifer Dorian, TNT, personal interviews, Feb.–Apr. 2002.

35ff   Steve Koonin, TNT, personal interviews, Feb.–Apr. 2002.

35ff   Scot Safon, TNT, personal interviews, Feb.–Apr. 2002.

Chapter 4. The Factual Channel

45   *CIA World Factbook: The World Factbook 2001,* Central Intelligence Agency, <http://www.cia.gov/cia/publications/factbook/>.

46   *Einstein quote:* <http://www.brainyquote.com/quotes/quotes/a/q109805.html>.

46   *Ivan Pavlov quote:* George Seldes, compiler, *The Great Thoughts* (New York: Ballantine, 1985), p. 326.

47   *Shenk quote:* David Shenk, *Data Smog: Surviving the Information Glut* (San Francisco: Harper Edge, 1997).

47   *Best quote:* Joel Best, *Damned Lies and Statistics: Untangling Numbers from the Media, Politicians, and Activists,* (Berkeley: Univ. of California Press, 2001), pp. 1ff.

48   *Children's Defense Fund:* Joel Best, <u>Damned Lies and Statistics</u>, pp. 1ff.

48   *"Crack the CEO code":* *Wall Street Journal,* March 27, 1995, editorial page.

49   *Paul O'Neill interview:* NBC, *Meet the Press,* Bob Somerby, "Our Current Howler (part II): Why Bother?" commentary in *The Daily Howler,* <http://www.dailyhowler.com/h030601_1.shtml>, March 6, 2001.

50ff   *Buzz Price:* personal interview, March 12, 2002.

52   *Chip Heath quote:* Kathleen O'Toole, "What Makes Some Ideas Hang Around," *Stanford Business,* February 2002, Volume 70, Number 2.

53   *Bill Gates quote:* <http://www.annemiller.com/article-make_that_selling_point_stick.html>.

53   *McNealy quote:* Scott McNealy, "Businesses built on Metaphors still need value," <http://www.sun.com/executives/perspectives/metaphors.html>. (This article originally appeared in Forbes ASAP, October 2000.)

53   *Article about KDD:* <http://www.kdnuggets.com/>.

53   *Lockbox and Fuzzy Math:* Chip Heath, Chris Bell, and Emily Sternberg, "Emotional Selection in Memes: The Case of Urban Legends," *Journal of Personality and Social Psychology* (Vol. 81), 2001.

53   *Fredrick R. Barnard quote:* Daryl Hepting, "What's a Picture Really Worth?" March 1999, <http://www.cs.uregina.ca/~hepting/proverbial/>.

53   *Lou Gilligan:* personal interview, June 1992.

54   *Railroad widths:* "Modern Engineering Design Principles: Dimensions in Time," <http://math.ucsd.edu/~kowalski/kowalski/math/humor/applied/HorsesButt.html>; Cecil Adams, "Was standard railroad gauge (4'8") determined by Roman chariot ruts?" Feb. 18, 2000, <http://www.straight

dope.com/columns/000218.html>; and "Ancient Romans and the Space Shuttle," <http://www.ivygreen.ctc.edu/luckmann/Challenges/A%20R&shuttle.htm>.

54   *Tufte quote:* Edward R. Tufte, *The Visual Display of Quantitative Data* (Cheshire, Conn.: Graphics Press, 1983), and Venkat Rajamanickam, March 8, 2001, "Visual Design for Instructional Content (Part I)," <http://www.elearningpost.com/elthemes/visual1.asp>.

55   *Thomas Peluso:* personal interview, May 1996.

56   *87 percent of all sales leads:* "Amazing Facts about Sales," March 3, 2002, <http://www.advance-sales.com/amazing_facts.htm>.

56   *More than 90 percent of all HIV infections:* Carol Ezzell, "Care For a Dying Continent," *Scientific American,* May 2000.

56   *The Centers for Disease Control reports:* Nicholas S. Martin, "What Does 'Iatrogenic' Mean?", <http://www.iatrogenic.org/index.html>.

CHAPTER 5. THE EMOTIONAL CHANNEL

62   *Bartelett and Ghoshal:* Christopher Bartlett and Sumantra Ghoshal, *Sloan Management Review,* winter 2002, Vol. 43, No. 2, "Building Competitive Advantage through People," p. 39.

62   *Drucker quote:* Peter Drucker, *Harvard Business Review*, February 2002, "They're Not Employees, They're People," pp. 70-77.

62   *Anita Roddick:* Anita Roddick, "Article for the Observer," <http://www.the-body-shop.com/global/news/anita_article.asp>.

63   *Jim Wright:* Jim Wright, *Reflections of a Public Man* (Madison Publishing, 1984).(Ft. Worth, Tex.: Allied Printing), p. 88.

63   *Kouzes and Posner:* James M. Kouzes and Barry Z. Posner, *The Leadership Challenge: How to Keep Getting Extraordinary Things Done in Organizations* (San Francisco: Jossey-Bass, 1995).

65   *Learned Optimism:* Martin E. P. Seligman, *Learned Optimism: How To Change Your Mind and Your Life* (New York: Knopf, 1991), pp. 97-106.

65   *Tom Peters: BusinessWeek,* November 16, 1992, Book Reviews.

65   *Tom Peters:* Dinesh D'Souza, *The Virtue of Prosperity: Finding Values in an Age of Techno-affluence* (New York: Free Press, 2000).

66   *Voltaire quote:* <http://www.cas.ucf.edu/english/publications/benson/quote5.htm>.

66   *Gardner quote:* Howard Gardner, *Frames of Mind: The Theory of Multiple Intelligences* (New York: Basic Books, 1983), p. 239.

67   *Dave Browne quotes:* personal interview, April 8, 9, 2002.

67   *Jamieson quotes:* Kathleen Hall Jamieson, *Eloquence in an Electronic Age: The Transformation of Political Speechmaking* (New York: Oxford Univ. Press, 1988), p. 182.

68   *Ronald Regan quote:*
    <http://enquirer.com/editions/2001/12/09/tem_crenna_searches_for.html>.

68   *Immelt quote:* <http://www.ge.com/news/immelt/europe.htm>.

69   *Fiorina quote:*
    <http://www.hp.com/hpinfo/execteam/speeches/fiorina/
goldman_02.htm>.

69   *Greatbatch and Clark:* David Greatbatch and Timothy Clark, *Humor and Laughter in the Public Lectures of Management Gurus,* research project, electronic copy.

70   *Don Clarke:* personal interview, April 30, 2002.

70   *Colin Powell:* Colin Powell, "A Leadership Primer,"
    <http://www.prm.nau.edu/prm426/colin_powells_leadership.htm>,
May 10, 2002.

70   *HayGroup survey:* Fabio Sala, "It's Lonely at the Top: Executives' Emotional Intelligence Self (Mis) Perceptions," <http://ei.haygroup.com/resources/
Library_articles/EI%20Feedback%20WP2.doc>, p. 4.

CHAPTER 6. THE SYMBOLIC CHANNEL

74   *McConkie and Parry:* Joseph F. McConkie and Donald W. Parry, *A Guide to Scriptural Symbols* (Salt Lake City: Bookcraft, 1990), p. 1.

74   *Tattersall quotes:* Ian Tattersall, *Scientific American,* December 2001, p. 61.

76   *WebMD quote:* WebMD Health, "Premenstrual Syndrome,"
    <http://my.webmd.com/encyclopedia/article/1680.51769>.

76   *Heather Shirley:* personal interview, March 8, 2002.

77   *Norm Dwyer quote:* personal interview, March 8, 2002.

77   *Mighty Midols:* The Mighty Midols,
    <http://www.midol.com/mightymidol/mightymidol.cfm>.

80   *Ted Mercer quote:*
    <http://www.aetc.randolph.af.mil/pa/AETCNS/Jul2001/01-140.htm>.

81   *Leo Burnett:* <http://www.leoburnett.com/nav/credentials.html>.

81   *Army of One ad campaign:* Bob Garfield, "Advertising Triumphs and Travesties, 2001: Looking Back at an Extraordinary Year," Advertising Age's AdReview, Dec. 31, 2001,
    <http://www.adreview.com/article.cms?articleId=871>.

82   *U.S. Army "Army of One":* U.S. Army, Question & Answer,
    <http://www.usarec.army.mil/launchkit/q_and_a/>.

83   *Churchill cigar:* TopCubans.com, "Romeo Y Julieta,"
    <http://www.topcubans.com/shop/cigars/romeo/>.

84   *MacArthur and National Guard:* Jean Darby, *Douglas MacArthur* (Minneapolis: Lerner Publications, c1989), and Douglas MacArthur, *Reminiscences* (New York: McGraw-Hill, 1964).

86   *Damasio quote:* Antonio R. Damasio, *The Feeling of What Happens: Body and Emotion in the Making of Consciousness* (New York: Harcourt Brace, 1999), p. 189.

86   *Sacks quote:* Oliver W. Sacks, *The Man Who Mistook His Wife for a Hat and Other Clinical Tales* (New York: Summit Books, 1985), p. 184.

87   *Marilyn Carlson Nelson quote:* <http://www.diversityjournal.com/ceospeeches/speech014.htm>.

88, 89 *Jody Lewis,* personal interview, April, 2000.

CHAPTER 7. THE SOUND OF SILOS

93   *Robin Dunbar:* Robin I. M. Dunbar, *Grooming, Gossip and the Evolution of Language* (Cambridge, Mass.: Harvard Univ. Press, 1998).

95   *Bob Galvin:* various interviews with authors, 1989 to 1994.

95, 96 *Crimson Tide,* 1995, all narrative transcribed from video by Don Simpson/Jerry Bruckheimer films in association with Hollywood Pictures.

98ff   *Alec Fraser:* personal interview, April 4, 2002.

101   *Bob Lutz's "great design":* Bob Lutz, "Speed Record: How GM Supercharged the Solstice Launch," *Popular Science,* May 2002, p. 54ff.

101   *Jack Rouse quote:* personal interview, May 13, 2002.

101   *Bill Gore:* <http://www.gore.com/about/culture.html>.

103   *Quadracci quote:* Harry Quadracci, *Thriving on Chaos,* Tom Peters videotape, 1989, Excel.

CHAPTER 8. WITHOUT WAX

108   *Maslow quote:* Abraham Maslow, *Toward a Psychology of Being* (Princeton, N.J.: Van Nostrand, 1962).

110   *Iain Morris:* personal interview, May, 1994.

111   *Peter Koestenbaum:* personal interview, October 10, 1993.

111   *Leo Tolstoy letter:* Letter from Leo Tolstoy to Valery Arsenev, dated 11/9/1856, quoted by Henri Troyat in *Tolstoy,* trans. Nancy Amphoux (Garden City, N.Y.: Doubleday, 1967), p. 156.

112   *Koestenbaum quote:* Peter Koestenbaum, *Leadership: The Inner Side of Greatness; A Philosophy for Leaders* (San Francisco: Jossey-Bass, 1991), p. 56.

112   *Eleanor Roosevelt quote:* Laurence J. Peter, compiler, *Peter's Quotations: Ideas for Our Times,* (New York: Quill/Morrow, 1992).

112   *Kets de Vries quote:* Manfred F. R. Kets de Vries, *Leaders, Fools and Impostors: Essays on the Psychology of Leadership* (San Francisco: Jossey-Bass, 1993), p. 179.

112   *Carl Rogers quote:* <http://www.dailycelebrations.com/change.htm>.

113   *High/low trusters:* Roderick M. Kramer, "Trust and Distrust in Organizations: Emerging Perspective, Enduring Questions," *Annual Review of Psychology* (1999) 50:569-98.

114   *Ailes quote:* Roger Ailes with Jon Kraushar, *You Are the Message: Secrets of the Master Communicators* (New York: Doubleday, 1988), preface.

116   *Garrison Keillor quote:*
       <http://www.brainyquote.com/quotes/quotes/g/q137096.html>.

118   *Argyris quote:* Chris Argyris, *Flawed Advice and the Management Trap: How Managers Can Know When They're Getting Good Advice and When They're Not* (New York: Oxford Univ. Press, 2000).

119   *"Antonio":* personal interview (names have been changed), March 15, 2002.

120,121 *Don Pierce,* personal interview, June, 1996, and May 10, 2002.

121   *Kets de Vries quote: Leaders, Fools and Impostors,* pp. 184-85.

CHAPTER 9. THE LADDER OF ABSTRACTION

126   *Arab proverb:* Peter Schwartz, *The Art of the Long View: Planning for the Future in an Uncertain World* (Doubleday, 1996), p. 52.

126   *Brand quote:* Stewart Brand, *The Clock of the Long Now: Time and Responsibility: The Ideas Behind the World's Slowest Computer* (New York: Basic Books, 2000), p. 34.

127   *Wishard quote:* William Van Dusen Wishard, *Between Two Ages: The 21st Century and the Crisis of Meaning* ([U.S.A.]: Xlibris Corporation), 2000.

127   *Paradigm shifts:* Ray Kurzweil, *The Age of Spiritual Machines: When Computers Exceed Human Intelligence* (New York: Penguin, 2000).

128   *Inamori quote:* Schwartz, *The Art of the Long View,* p. 66.

129   *Jamieson quote:* Jamieson, *Eloquence in an Electronic Age,* p. 239.

131   *Gardner quote:* John W. Gardner, *Self-Renewal: The Individual and the Innovative Society* (New York: Harper & Row, 1965), p. 98.

131   *Lumet quote:* Sidney Lumet, *Making Movies,* (New York: Vintage Books, 1996), p. 136.

135   *Mitchell quote:* Colin Mitchell, "Selling the Brand Inside," *Harvard Business Review,* January 2002.

136   *The LEGO Group vision and values:*
       <http://www.lego.com/eng/info/values.asp>,
       <http://www.lego.com/eng/info/values/businessarea.asp,
       <http://www.lego.com/eng/info/values/creativity.asp>,
       <http://www.lego.com/eng/info/values/vision.asp>,
       <http://www.lego.com/eng/info/history.asp>, all sites accessed May 10, 2002.

137ff *Henderson quote:* Ronald H. Henderson Jr., "Capt. Ronald H. Henderson, Jr., Commanding Officer USS John F. Kennedy (CV 67), IMC Remarks to JFK Crew, 10 March 2002," used with permission.

CHAPTER 10. ONE VOICE

143ff *Dave Browne:* interview, April 8, 9, 2002.

144 *Ezra Benson Taft quote:* <http://www.mindonfire.com/default.asp?page=4>, accessed May 10, 2002.

144 *Harley-Davidson quote:* David Ulrich, Jack Zenger, and Norm Smallwood, *Results-Based Leadership* (Boston: Harvard Business School Press, 1999), p. 38.

145 *Jayne-Anne Gadhia:* interview, March 10, 2002.

146 *Peter Drucker quote:* "Step 7: Demonstrate Leadership," <http://www.actlikeanowner.com/page.cfm?Page_ID=329>.

146 *Senge quote:* Peter Senge, *The Fifth Discipline: The Art & Practice of The Learning Organization* (New York: Doubleday, 1990), p. 346.

146 *Bob Chambers:* Bob Chambers, It's Alive Co., personal interview, May 7, 2002.

147 *Scott Givens:* Scott Givens, Salt Lake Olympic Organizing Committee, personal interviews, March 12 and March 27, 2002.

147 *Mitt Romney:* Mitt Romney, Salt Lake Olympic Organizing Committee, personal interview, May 6, 2002.

149 *Haven Riviere:* Haven Riviere, personal interview, April 8, 2002.

149 *Salt Lake Games results:* Lisa Riley Roche and Brady Snyder, "Games reap big profits for Salt Lake," *Deseret News,* May 3, 2002.

149 *Lloyd Ward quote:* Richard Sandomir, "As Games End, Marketing Games Begin," *New York Times,* Feb. 28, 2002.

149 *Salt Lake Games results:* Lisa Riley Roche, "Games surplus no $80 million," *Deseret News,* April 22, 2002.

149 *Salt Lake Games results:* Dave Anderton, "Hotels rode high on Oly business," *Deseret News,* March 29, 2002.

149 *Salt Lake Games results:* Dave Anderton, "Olympic impact," *Deseret News,* March 3, 2002.

149 *Salt Lake Games results:* "Games-related economic development numbers," *Deseret News,* March 2, 2002.

149 *Salt Lake Games results:* Lisa Riley Roche, "Ebersol rates S.L. Games tops," *Deseret News,* February 27, 2002.

149 *Salt Lake Games results:* Jerry D. Spangler and Bob Bernick Jr., "SLOC repays the state $59 million," *Deseret News,* February 26, 2002.

150 *Fraser Bullock quote:* Lisa Riley Roche, Associated Press, "Mitt inflates Games role, paper says," *Deseret News,* April 1, 2002.

LAST WORD: CALLING ALL CAPITALISTS

153 *Gardner quote:* John W. Gardner, *On Leadership* (New York: Free Press, 1990), p. 8.

154 *Boston Globe quote:* Thomas Farragher and Alice Dembner, "Lax, outdated systems at root of INS troubles," *Boston Globe,* September 30, 2001.

156   *Petroski quote:* Henry Petroski, *To Engineer Is Human: The Role of Failure in Successful Design* (New York: Vintage Books, 1992).

157   *Goldberger quote:* Paul Goldberger, "The Sameness of Things," *The New York Times Magazine,* April 6, 1997, pp. 56-60.

157   *Nordström/Ridderstråle quote:* Kjell Nordström and Jonas Ridderstråle, *Funky Business: Talent Makes Capital Dance,* Financial Times (New York: Prentice Hall, 2000).

158   *Dr. William Haseltine quote:* Jeff Fischer and Tom Jacobs, "Immortality Could Be Possible," The Motley Fool, Fool.com, <http://www.fool.com/portfolios/rulebreaker/2001/rulebreaker010308.htm>, March 8, 2001.

158   *De Soto quote:* Hernando de Soto, *The Mystery of Capital: Why Capitalism Triumphs in the West and Fails Everywhere Else* (New York: Basic Books, 2000), p. 7.

159   *De Soto quote: The Mystery of Capital,* p. 227.

CREDITS

www.theleadersvoice.biz

tompeters! company

Authors Boyd Clarke and Ron Crossland are the CEO and vice chair of tompeterscompany!. Founded in the 1980s by renowned author and management guru Tom Peters, the global company helps organizations introduce, implement, and integrate learning for extraordinary results. Over the years, the company has worked with hundreds of clients. Nearly 300,000 people have attended tompeterscompany! workshops, including the company's four main product offerings:

The Leadership Challenge™ Workshop
Developed by Jim Kouzes and Barry Posner, The Leadership Challenge™ Workshop is the gold standard for leadership development training and offers a stellar track record in practice. Based on the best-selling book *The Leadership Challenge,* this workshop teaches The Five Practices™ leaders follow to achieve remarkable success. Based on rock-solid research, these practices are Modeling the Way, Inspiring a Shared Vision, Challenging the Process, Enabling Others to Act, and Encouraging the Heart.

The Leader's Voice™ Workshop
Even before this book was published, Boyd Clarke and Ron Crossland were teaching the principles of The Leader's Voice™. This workshop helps leaders create passionate alignment by communicating with Facts, Emotions, and Symbols. It focuses on the principles of communication rather than polish and presence. Those who attend will achieve better alignment around key strategic initiatives, improved productivity spurred by higher levels of trust, higher morale triggered by an understandable vision, increased efficiency, and better communication by all throughout the organization.

WOW!Projects™ Workshop
Designed to transform any project into a Wow! project, this workshop is based on Tom Peters' book *the project50.* It shows employees how to shape any project (critical or mundane) into projects that are WOW!, memorable, and make a difference. At the WOW!Projects™ Workshop, participants will engage in fast prototyping, learn how to generate bigger ideas, assess team roles through the Belbin Team Role Inventory, focus on maximizing the impact of projects for clients, and discover ways to garner more support and buy-in for projects.

Brand Inside: Brand Outside™ Workshop
Most organizations ignore Brand Inside and instead focus their large brand investment outside on advertising, marketing, product positioning, and so on. However, by ensuring a brand is clearly defined to, valued by, and expressed by each employee, companies can seize the opportunity to create a positive brand experience. Brand Inside is a key branding opportunity with customers because employees impact customers the most. This workshop shows companies how to effectively bring the Brand Inside!

For more information on how tompeterscompany! can help your organization, please visit www.tompeters.com or call 513.683.4702.